WATERLOO

Relics

Gilles Bernard & Gérard Lachaux

translated from the French by Alan McKay

Histoire & Collections

In memory of our fathers
André and Fernand

INTRODUCTION

"Waterloo, morne plaine..." (Waterloo, sad plain). These three words still echo in French people's minds. Beyond Victor Hugo's writings, they remember that it was a defeat rather than a battle and also, depending on where your opinions lie, the final act of a fantastic epic or that of a terrible despot.

Hougoumont, Mont-Saint-Jean, who remembers them? To be fair there are far more amateurs of history than one can imagine, even in France! And even if on the English side of the Channel, the memory of the event is commemorated more, this is not just to celebrate a decisive victory, but mainly to honour the memory of their ancestors. This common culture, which is more or less fervent with some than with others, has brought thousands of Europeans on the roads to this "sad plain". They take in at a glance the area of rich soil where more than 40 000 men fell in a single day.

Each in their own manner, painters, artists and writers more or less successfully and objectively created works for posterity in the decades following the slaughter. The representations of the battle painted by Philippoteaux, Croft or Hillingford, including the impressive panorama by Robiquet, Malespina and Desvarreux painted in 1911 are their versions of a battle relived in their own minds, their interpretation of the facts which even down to the smallest details in the end will never be wholly authentic.

As for the writings, the memoirs came first, then the historical studies. These fill entire libraries just by themselves. Among the most well-known, Siborne, Winand Aerts, Houssaye and Lachouque; they have expressed themselves for posterity. Anybody deeply interested in strategy can thus analyse the slightest phases of this terrible confrontation down to the tiniest details - each movement of the soldiers, each charge, each battery salvo... Untiringly, the war-game enthusiasts play out the battle over and over again, correct the loser's mistakes and crown him with the laurel wreaths of revenge. But to what use? History has already been written... Using lead soldiers then their plastic descendants, the opposing armies are made to relive the scenes again but in miniature this time. Talented Napoleon buffs - "Napoleonians" - with a vocation worthy of that of the great masters, reproduce the colours of yesteryear's uniforms.

But the fascination exerted by the plumes and the golden eagles, just as much as that exerted by the impeccable deployment of the richly-bedecked infantry squares and squadrons, runs the risk strangely enough of causing the buffs to forget one essential thing: the reality of the fighting, the inherent horrors of such wars. Has everything been done - painted, written, drawn – to remind people of that horror?

Authentic proof of the battle has had to be found at its source. Almost two centuries afterwards, the only valid proof, in our opinion, was those objects which had really "been" at Waterloo. Strangely enough, with all the books and publications on the subject, nobody ever seemed to have taken an interest in this aspect. And yet their emotional capital still remains intact, from the very famous hat belonging to Napoleon to the uniform button of an obscure infantry fusilier.

The official museums and the private collections conceal a host of these objects. Old trophies picked up after the fighting, piously preserved family heirlooms passed down from generation to generation. Analysing these relics minutely often teaches us that there are many things which are not taught in the history books.

Finally the battlefield itself continues to give up the last true witnesses of this tragedy which has almost become a legend. Thus in the space of an instant, seeing a handful of bullets all covered in clay from the furrows enables one to imagine in the empty distant plain, from Mont-Saint-Jean to the Belle-Alliance, that huge crowd of vanished armies...

A MECCA FOR REMEMBRANCE

Waterloo, 1826, eleven years after the battle, those who defeated Napoleon decided to make the Mont-Saint-Jean an important place for the memory of the fallen. With a sense of the grandiose never equalled later, the Netherlands set the tone. At the very spot where the Prince of Orange was wounded the Butte du Lion (the Heights of the lion) was built after three years' work. It is an imposing 130 feet high hillock on which the statue of the lion seems tiny in spite of weighing 28 tonnes. To match this historical event, the monument is visible from miles away. It is also an ideal observation post. After climbing the 226 steps, the visitor – can we already speak of tourists? – discovers the whole battlefield.

The same year, a man built a hotel at the foot of the Butte du Lion. This was ex-Sergeant-Major Cotton, a former trooper of the 7th Hussars in Wellington's army. He devoted the rest of his life to perpetuating the memory of the battle and very quickly imposed himself as the guide and historian of the place. He sought and found a number of relics from the fighting but more among the local inhabitants than on the battlefield; they were picked up during the days following the battle. Over the years, he constituted a real museum where arms, military head gear, items of equipment and miscellaneous bits of copper piled up, all witnesses of the great fight in 1815.

This original initiative begot success. A lot of mainly British veterans of the battle visited the site and this was profitable for the owner of the property. The precious eyewitness accounts which he gathered from them helped him to perfect his knowledge of events, which he exploited by publishing his own story of the battle in 1846: "A Voice from Waterloo". The Mont-Saint-Jean guide died in 1849 at the age of 57 and was buried at Hougoumont at the very place where his compatriots had distinguished themselves 34 years earlier. His descendants continued to care for the museum whose reputation soon encouraged the beginning of a small trade in souvenirs. "An interesting collection of memorabilia guaranteed as really being from the Waterloo campaign, of which some are labelled for sale at a moderate price, although they are not as cheap as the fakes which abound in the neighbourhood". Would Sergeant Cotton have allowed this? In 1896, the Barral Guide mentions this trade without beating about the bush. "From time to time, the plough unearths small objects such as bits of weapons, buttons, parts of skeletons, etc. But when the salesmen run out of stock, they worry about resorting to other sources. It seems that most of the relics which are sold to the insatiable English are shipped every spring from a factory in Birmingham which has large contracts with these special Waterloo shops." In 1909, the owner decided to sell the hotel and the museum, whose contents was dispersed during a huge public sale in Brussels. More than 3 000 historical items disappeared, nearly all of them into private collections the world over. If Cotton's work did not survive the first years of the 20th century, his name however remains attached to the story of Waterloo and to a praiseworthy attempt to serve its memory both in writing and with artefacts.

The Butte du Lion.
Photo Gérard Lachaux, Rights Reserved

Victors are naturally inclined to return to the place where they triumphed. But for each of the 1815 Allies, the Waterloo battlefield had a different significance. For the Prussians, their country's new found identity occurred on the plain of Leipzig in 1813 and this remains the important symbol. The Dutch and the Belgians consider this campaign as the only expression of an apparent national unity which already carried in it the seeds of the 1830 Revolution. But it was not the same for the English who, for the occasion, included the Scots, the Welsh and the Irish in their name. Waterloo marks the end of their country's struggle to the death against Revolutionary France. All the famous English officers, among them the most important, the Duke of Wellington, made the pilgrimage to this corner of Brabant. In the early months following the campaign, a trend started which never stopped. In 1815 Walter Scott, followed a year later by Lord Byron made the journey, imitated by an anonymous multitude of His Majesty's subjects. On the other hand, despite the interest shown in the tragedy following the fall of the Empire, for a long time to the French, Waterloo seemed to be detached from the reality of the site. Victor Hugo, the wandering exile wrote his famous "Waterloo, Waterloo, Morne plaine" in 1852 without ever visiting the battlefield, even though he had lived for several months in Brussels the year before. It was only nine years later that he visited the site but only for the purposes of the chapter in his book, "les Misérables", devoted to the tragedy.

Below.
La Haie-Sainte after Montius. This engraving which shows what the farm looked like a short while after the events, already displays the commemorative plaque dedicated to the officers of the 2nd Light Battalion of the King's German Legion who had fallen within its walls. This marble lozenge was set up on the wall along the road by their comrades as early as September 1815.
Musée Wellington Collection, Waterloo.

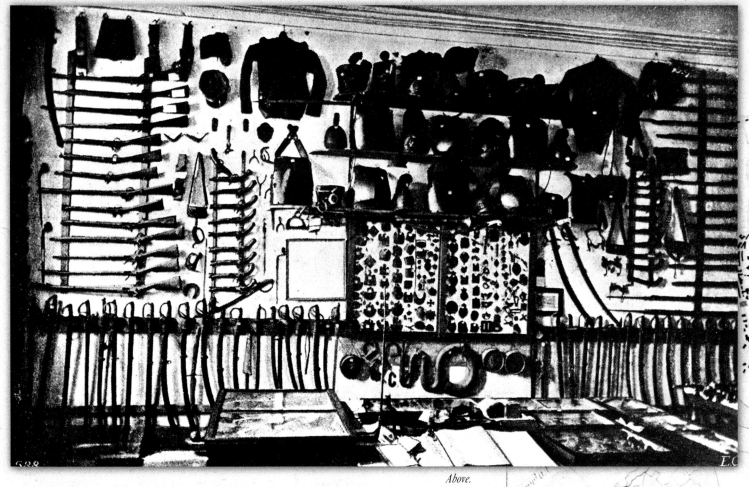

Above.

One aspect of the Cotton Collection at the beginning of the 20th century. Since the death of its creator in 1849, the museum continued to prosper. But a lot of the items which were donated by private people turned out never to have been used in the fighting at Waterloo and thus rather spoilt the exhibition of authentic objects. For example, two English soldiers'uniforms which are now in the Musée Royal de l'Armée in Brussels and which belonged to units which did not take part in the battle. On the other hand certain objects were certified as authentic. For instance, in the impressive collection of sabres was the one belonging to General Alexander MacDonald who was wounded during the battle. The weapon lost in 1815 was recognised by its former owner when he visited the Hotel at Mont-Saint-Jean. Inside the glass case full of shako plates and miscellaneous copper items, there is also a strange wind instrument called a"serpent"and several English flasks whose origin is not in doubt… No one would have thought of bringing one from somewhere else. Almost all the rifles which were collected in the region had been converted for hunting by sawing off the barrel and the stock. The fact that modest people re-used what remained after the battle was one of the main factors which helped to recover the items.

Private Collection.

Right.
This An IX-model French
Light Cavalry Sabre also belonged
to the rich collection at Mont-Saint-Jean
and was rediscovered again in the USA.
Sergeant-Major Cotton might have even fixed the little chain
to the leather loops of the scabbard himself
when dressing one of his dummies.
Musée Wellington Collection, Waterloo.

PLAN DE LA BATAILLE
DE
WATERLO
ou de Mont-St-Jea

PAR W. B. CRAA

"A voice from Waterloo": this book published by Edward Cotton in 1840 remained the reference work for along time for anybody interested in the battle. Translated into French in 1874, it went through several editions. It is here shown on a map printed in 1840 after that drawn up in 1816 by the Belgian Engineer, Craan. *Private Collection.*

This French shako from the old Cotton collection
was bought recently in the USA
by the Wellington Museum at Waterloo.
To begin with there is some doubt that
the hat was actually used in 1815. However,
the use of the 1806 plaque was most probable
because in order to reconstitute the Imperial
Army in only a few weeks, all the means that were
available were used. Now, it no longer matters what
the regulations said, provided that this "cuckoo" has
returned to its nest again. Moreover,
a similar type of plaque was found on the battlefield.

Musée Wellington Collection, Waterloo.

Below.
Photographed form the Butte du Lion, the Museum Hotel
at Mont-Saint-Jean as it was at the beginning of the 20th century.
The village of Waterloo is on the horizon. The tourists from across
the Channel could not miss the famous hotel and its English bar. Moreover
a wall painted with big letters reminds them that here
was founded "the oldest true museum".
Private Collection.

524 — Panorama de la Plaine de WATERLOO. Vue sur Waterloo et le Mont Saint-Jean. ND Phot.

AN INEXHAUSTIBLE SUBJECT

On the morrow of the battle, those who had taken part, foremost among them the Emperor, gave their version of events. As early as 1818, Napoleon started the argument by saying that his lieutenants were responsible for the defeat. These men did not want to be out-done and Grouchy and Gérard tore each other apart in their corre-spondence. Then it was the historians' turn and they gave their own conception of the facts, depending on their political inclinations. Thiers and Charras thus had very different ideas about the campaign. The Napoleonic legend had its stalwart defenders and its talented detractors. Decades passed and the quarrel, although put back into its context by Houssaye, Lachouque or Marguerit has still not been set-tled. For the English, Siborne's writings were the authority for a long time. Everybody gave their opinion from their own nationality's point of view in order to defend their countrymen's role. But there is one domain in which these endless debates always contribute something positive: the battlefield itself. Here, when somebody important evokes the battle, this raises an army of... tourists ready to take up arms like yesterday's soldiers. Because of this success, all sorts of productions with artistic or historical pretensions, or even more banal commercial activi-ties, see the light of day so that some people actually are actual-ly able to live off the memories of Waterloo.

Below.
"*To the last combatants of the Grande Armée*". On 28 June 1904, five years before the demise of the Cotton Museum, the French officially marked their return to the site which held so many memories for them by inaugurating their own monument. A huge crowd, estimated by the authorities at more than 100 000 people crowed the place. Never since 1815 had the battlefield been occupied by so many people in a single day. Only a few years before, scarcely 200 French people made the pilgrimage every year compared with almost eight thousand Britons and more than three thousand Americans!
Private Collection.

Inauguration du Monument Français à Waterloo (28 Juin 1904).

Waterloo

Les monuments

Left.
One of the countless post cards of the Waterloo monuments sold in Belgium at the very beginning of the 20th century. With the Butte du Lion in the background, one can see the Monument to the Hanoverians and that of Colonel Gordon, Wellington's aide de camp, mortally wounded on that spot on 18 June.
Private Collection.

Nels, Bruxelles Serie 11 No. 640

9

Left.
When History brings prosperity…
A menu from the restaurant at the sunken lane
at Ohain handed out over a century ago.
Private Collection.

Below.
Well before the post card was invented,
photographers took pictures of the battlefield for the amateurs.
This shot taken in 1860 shows Hougoumont,
almost unchanged since a certain 18 June…
Private Collection.

Above.

A version of the Imperial cavalry's charges. This sketch by the painter Henri Georges Chartier gives an enthusiastic view of these glorious assaults. After the fall of the Second Empire, Waterloo became a favourite subject for French military painters. Intending to exorcise the cruel 1870-71 war, the artists appealed to the memory of the Emperor's last battle. Grandeur and glory could be expressed by illustrating episodes from the ultimate defeat. The Napoleonic legend thus helped the suffering country to recover its national pride.

Laurent Mirouze Collection.

Blood was spilt,
ink replaced it…
Such is the way with History
and historians.
Photo Gérard Lachaux,
Rights Reserved.

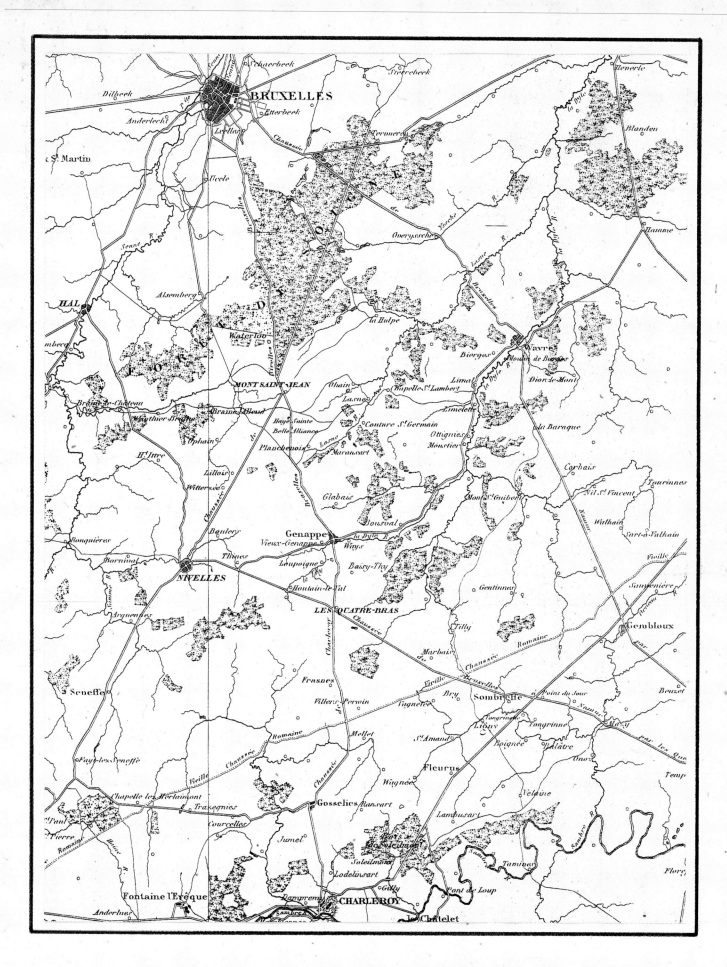

Map of the Waterloo region after the atlas by Thiers. The fate of all Europe was played out between Brussels and Charleroi in four days.
Private Collection.

In Brussels, at the end of the 19th century, the French painter Charles Castellani painted an admirable Panorama. This fascicule, printed at the time was intended for visitors. In his memoirs "Confidences d'un panoramiste" (Confidences of a panorama painter), the artist tells the following story to explain why his work has been forgotten: *"The Waterloo panorama which went to London afterwards was a complete fiasco and this can be easily explained. I had painted the battle as it stood at 5 p.m. when the battle was in full swing and when our soldiers seemed to be about to win. It was a real apotheosis for Napoleon I, who could be seen on his horse in the middle of his legendary square, with a ray of sunlight filtering through the stormy sky onto his head."*

Private Collection.

PANORAMA NATIONAL

BATAILLE DE WATERLOO

par Charles CASTELLANI

PLAN ET DESCRIPTION

Bruxelles, Boulevard du Hainaut, Place Fontainas

Le soir tombait, la lutte était ardente et noire.
...vait l'offensive et presque la victoire.
...tenait Wellington acculé contre un bois,
...lunette à la main, il observa : parfois
...centre du combat, point obscur où tressaille
...mêlée effroyable et vivante broussaille,
...parfois l'horizon sombre comme la mer ;
...dain, joyeux il dit : Grouchy ! c'était Blucher.
V. Hugo.

... Panorama a été construite d'après
...QUEZ, architecte, à Bruxelles ; les
...UR.

ITINÉRAIRES E. FLAMMARION

GEORGES BARRAL

ITINÉRAIRE ILLUSTRÉ

DE

L'ÉPOPÉE DE WATERLOO

ERNEST FLAMMARION, ÉDITEUR

In 1896, Georges Barral who had already written an "Epopée de Waterloo" (a Waterloo epic) made up from unpublished writings and the memories of both his grand-fathers, had Flammarion publish a guide of the battlefield for tourists. This interesting little book which is very difficult to find nowadays, is full of anecdotes about the inhabitants' lucrative exploitation of the site.

Private Collection.

NAPOLEON

In the Gulf of Juan on 1 March 1815, in the pale early morning light, a rather strange, although familiar – especially in the region – gathering walked along the beach. At the head of his tiny 1 200-man army, Napoleon was once again on French soil which he had left less than a year previously. He made an eloquent proclamation explaining his gesture to the inhabitants bemused by his return. "You reproach me for sacrificing the greater interest of the Motherland to my own rest. I have crossed the seas through all sorts of dangers; I have come among you to take back my rights, which are also yours."

Twenty days later, in the twentieth year of his reign, Louis XVIII was fleeing and the Emperor entered the Tuileries after reconquering France without shedding a drop of blood. After an incredible rise to power over less than twenty years, the man who had lived through enough to fill a hundred lifetimes had once again taken control of his destiny.

His fall from power in 1814 had been a terrible experience for the former master of Europe. Abandoned, betrayed, even by death which did not want him, the Emperor of the French, King of Italy, Protector of the Confederation of the Rhine and Mediator of the Swiss Federation, had become the Sovereign of the Island of Elba. The supreme irony of it was that the Treaty of Fontainebleau had left him with the title of Emperor of this derisory piece of land.

But a finale of this sort was not for such a man.

But what was the reason of this, his latest attempt? Did Napoleon believe that the Empire could be restored in a lasting way? Without doubt, "No", as he later confessed at St Helena. "*I felt my good fortune abandoning me. I no longer had that feeling of being successful indefinitely…*" Was it a question therefore of making a good exit, in front of the whole world? Some have defended this idea, even declaring that the drama at Waterloo does not belong to the History of France but only to Napoleon Bonaparte's biography.

So why? Why all this unbelievable activity in giving the country new institutions, reconstituting the Imperial Army and preparing for war, a war which was made all the more inevitable by the frightening return of the man whom the Sovereigns had outlawed at the Vienna Congress? Can we not discern in him the will to set ablaze the old Europe one final time, so that the conflagration started by the French Revolution (of which he wanted to be the heir) would never be extinguished? If the convulsions which had shattered the old order and had for a while calmed down, if they were roused again all the work of the Empire would not be effaced. Was this the unlimited vanity or the superhuman genius of Napoleon? The question has been asked; anybody nowadays can try to form his own opinion. It is perhaps this rather vertiginous question mark which could explain the fascination which the Emperor's personal souvenirs hold for people ever since 1815. Through them they can approach the unfathomable mystery of an extraordinary being. Be they the relics venerated by those who worship the cult of the Emperor or the trophies picked up on the battlefield by yesterday's victors these objects, by means of some strange alchemy, have caused a sort of agitation among those who possess them. Without realising that they were responding to the same attraction, Napoleon's former enemies have also transmitted these silent witnesses of his fantastic destiny throughout the generations, one would say almost piously. From the most prestigious to the most obscure, some of them have come down to us in sometimes rather strange circumstances. For those who can see them today, they still transmit the same singular, still perceptible emotion.

Above.
Portrait of the Emperor painted during the Hundred Days by a talented miniaturist. There is an inscription on the other side "Approuvé par Isabey" (approved by Isabey), Napoleon's famous portraitist and painter of the original work.
Private Collection.

VENERATED OBJECTS

It is normal for the luxury and splendour which attends any monarch - even more so if he adopted the title of Emperor - to leave traces of the impressive magnificence which still affects us after all this time. Although the furniture, the numerous utensils and the ceremonial wardrobes of Napoleon's Imperial palaces are still a source of wonder, they are nevertheless nothing alongside the simpler legendary elements of his clothes. Amidst all the gold and rich trimmings, the only person visible is the one who did not wear any! Thanks to this particularity of his genius, the Emperor's personal effects are loaded with unequalled emotional appeal. It is the man himself who appears beneath the myth. Their association with those dramatic hours at Waterloo and their symbolic value express themselves even more powerfully.

Right.

The legendary frock coat. This was taken to Saint-Helena; it was cut in 1815 by the tailor, Lejeune, for the price of 15 francs, and worn by the Emperor during the Belgian Campaign. He gave it to Montholon and it was then bought by Napoleon III who had it placed in the "Musée des Souverains" in 1854.

Copyright Musée de l'Armée, Paris.

Below.

The hat worn by the Emperor at Waterloo must be without question the most emblematic of all the souvenirs of the 1815 Campaign. Misshapen by the rain and the storms of the 16th and 17th June it was sent to the hat-maker Poupart to be repaired as soon as Napoleon reached Paris. Indeed, thrifty as the Emperor was where his own wardrobe was concerned, he wanted his hats to be put back into shape as best as possible. But a few days later, the man who was not yet the outlaw of Saint-Helena was on the road to exile. Nobody came to claim the hat which in the end Poupart kept. It later became the property of General Duchesne, who donated it to the museum at Sens where it is today.

Collection in the Musée de Sens.
Photo J.P. Elie.

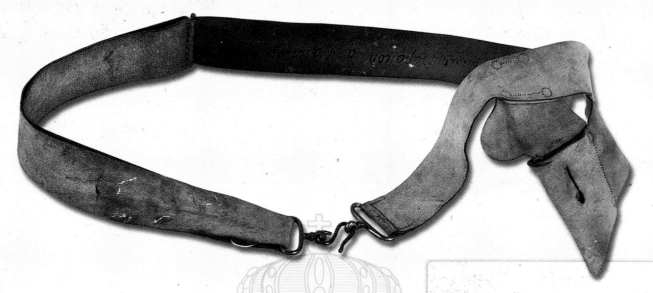

Above.

In the twilight of Waterloo, while all around him was collapsing, the Emperor put his hand
to his sword, seeming for a moment to want to seek death on the battlefield. But he was led away
by his entourage and made up his mind to leave that fateful place where his good luck had just run out.
The scabbard in which he put his sword - now forever beaten - was held by this white leather belt,
made by Saint-Etienne the Younger "Ceinturier de S.M. l'Empereur et Roi, de sa Maison et de celles des
Princes" (Belt maker to the Emperor and King, of his Household and those of the Princes).
A century later, this precious souvenir was listed in the military painter, Poilpot's impressive collection. In
February 1915, his widow offered it to General Gallieni. The Governor of Paris
did not want to keep this surprising present for his own personal pleasure so the same day, he sent
his aide de camp to offer it to the Musée de l'Armée where it still is.

Copyright Musée de l'Armée, Paris.

Below.

This richly worked bridle bit comes from the harness of one of the horses used by the Emperor.
Before the battlefield was concealed from view by the gun smoke, the Emperor could be seen very clearly
from the Allied lines, passing up and down in front of the French troops who acclaimed him. The great
leader mounted on his white horse was so familiar a sight that, according to Cotton (1)
"An English artillery officer ran up to the Duke of Wellington and said:
'Your Grace, I can see Napoleon very clearly accompanied by his headquarters staff;
my cannon are pointing in their very direction. Should I open fire?'
To which the Duke replied:
'Certainly not, I will not permit it;
it is not for commanding officers to go about shooting at each other.'"

Copyright Musée de l'Armée.

16

THE EMPEROR TOUCHED THEM...

There is also another category of souvenirs which has taken pride of place in what remains of the great man's effects. These are not the items tailored with the care that can be imagined for Napoleon's personal use but, on the contrary, items which he came across by pure chance. Nothing predestined that these ordinary utensils would enter History, and they would have disappeared naturally at the end of their allotted span. But in the space of one fleeting moment, they became the holders of the memory that the witnesses kept of those rather exceptional moments. The cult of the Emperor, which was to develop years later, thus found one of its most unexpected sources. Without exaggerating one could say that the mere fact that he touched these items made what was insignificant before his arrival into something sacred.

Below.
The episode at the Belle Vue bar by James Thiriar.
Musée Napoléon de Ligny Collection.

At the Belle Vue tavern built on the heights at the entrance to Charleroi where the Brussels road crosses the Fleurus road, at the beginning of the afternoon of 15 June 1815, the owner and his servants watched the continuous parade of French troops marching to meet the enemy with astonishment. In the continuous hammering of the horseshoes, Pajol's Hussar Corps were filing past the building when a group of horsemen suddenly entered the courtyard. An officer advanced and asked for a drink for his Majesty who had just dismounted. Everybody rushed forward. The owner of the bar could not believe his eyes and feverishly brought a glass and this pitcher full of cold water. After drinking, the sovereign relaxed on a chair which was brought for him. On the road, the Young Guard was passing by and the men, noticing Napoleon, acclaimed him noisily. The Emperor smiled and… fell asleep for a few moments amidst the cheering. From that day on this modest pitcher, suddenly given this unforeseen aura, was the proud property of the Belle Vue tavern which displayed it to the curiosity of its customers. Passed down from hand to hand, unfortunately broken then repaired with staples, it remains a silent witness to this amazing scene.

"Dernier quartier général de Napoléon" Collection.

Below.

At the entrance to Fleurus a woman handed the Emperor this pot full of stock. By dipping his lips into the liquid, the Sovereign, appreciative of the young woman's completely natural familiarity, offered her an unexpected treasure which she preserved piously. This poor pot became her most precious treasure and it was handed down generation after generation so that the memory would not die. The Napoleon Museum at Ligny is now the depository of this moving heritage.

Musée Napoléon de Ligny Collection.

Below.
Napoleon drank from this cup in a farm at Charleroi on the morning of 15 June. Because of this simple act, it is now forever associated with the memory of those tragic days.

Copyright Musée de l'Armée, Paris.

A PALACE AT LE CAILLOU

It was traditional to call all the places where the Emperor set up his headquarters "palaces". All during the Empire's campaigns, dozens of buildings even simple peasant huts sometimes were given this prestigious name. Situated along the road to Brussels le Caillou Farm welcomed the Sovereign's teams on the evening of 17 June. Within these walls, Napoleon thought he still held his destiny in his own hands. What he said was taken down by witnesses to the meal he took on the morning of the 18th, and is eloquent on the subject. *"The enemy's army is superior to ours by a quarter, we have nevertheless 90 per cent for us and not 10 against."* And the Emperor concluded: *"Gentlemen, if my orders are carried out scrupulously, we will sleep in Brussels tonight."* The owner of the farm, Henry Boucquéau, who was worried for his property, was well received by Napoleon who reassured him on his future. Less than twelve hours later, the unbelievable took place and the Sovereign's ruin caused that of the farmer.

Right.

Decorated with his portrait, this crystal carafe comes from the service used for the last time during the Emperor's meal on 18 June at about eight o'clock le Caillou. It is amazing that despite the frenzied manner with which the carriages were looted, such a fragile object should have survived intact. As surprising as it may seem, a second carafe has also survived, preserved in a private collection in Brussels.

Private Collection.

Below.
Le Caillou Farm after the battle, lithography by Taillois after Montius.
Although situated several miles from the battlefield, the farm was completely burnt down on the morning of the 19th. The victors' revenge did not spare this, the Emperor's last "Palace".
Wellington Museum Collection, Waterloo.

Above.

On this post card dating from the beginning of the 20th century, le Caillou Farm the last of the Emperor's headquarters. Behind the high walls of the orchard, the Chasseurs à pied of the 1st Battalion of the 1st Guards Regiment, commanded by Major Duuring camped in terrible weather, guarding the "palace" where the Emperor sheltered for the last time as a victorious leader. The road still looks like what it must have looked like at the time in 1815. It was along this sunken road enclosed between the banks that Wellington's retreating soldiers and their French pursuers marched on 17 June towards the "Belle Alliance". The following day, on the evening of the disaster, the same place witnessed the terrible rout of the fleeing Imperial army.

Private Collection.

Left.

The Emperor spent very little time on his meals, and even less when he was campaigning. But his kitchens were still nonetheless those of a Sovereign; they were very well organised and equipped with a lot of utensils. This little copper pan, stamped with the Imperial "N" was abandoned in the very place where it performed its function for the last meal.

"Dernier quartier général de Napoléon" Collection.

MAJOR VON KELLER'S
GOOD LUCK

Tales of the battle of Waterloo taken from a great variety of sources have given rise to legends which over the years have taken on the semblance of truth. The story of the capture of the Emperor's berlin by Major Heinrich Eugen Baron von Keller, of the Fusilier Battalion of the 15th Silesian Regiment is a good example. Normally, nothing predisposed a simple major in the Prussian army to have his name written in History. Yet, glory and fortune were up for grabs for any officer who was ready to seize the opportunity. When this arose, he knew how to get the best out it. It was proof that in the heat of victory, one had to remain cool-headed in order to be praised especially after telling tales. When legend is at that price, it is better to stick to reality.

Below.
A picture of one of the main curiosities of the Mme Tussaud's at the beginning of the 20th century. This carriage, incorrectly called a berlin since it is the easy carriage made by Goeting following an order in a few weeks in April 1815, had left the headquarters at le Caillou no doubt shortly before 8 p.m. when the number of fleeing soldiers announced that defeat was imminent. At the entrance of Genappe where an improvised barricade had

been erected across the road, the team could advance no further. Deciding to go round the village, the coachmen were not able to leave the road as the carriage had got stuck in the mud almost immediately. One Jean Hornn, claiming to be Napoleon's coachman has left a tale of the carriage's capture by the Prussian troops. He explains how he was cut down at his post (indeed he lost an arm) and left for dead by some cavalry. The berlin had disappeared when he came to and he managed to hide in a house nearby. Although his story seems to be true, it is nevertheless subject to caution. Indeed, his name does not appear on the roll of personnel assigned to the Emperor's carriage teams either in 1815 or even in 1814. Moreover, the job of coachman did not exist since this type of carriage was driven "en poste", i.e. by coachmen riding the team horses. The outside seat was kept for Napoleon's bodyguard, the Mameluke Ali. Arriving on the spot, Major von Keller immediately claimed the easy carriage as his prize. It seems certain, according to the witnesses, that the Baron got his hands on the diamonds that the Emperor had had bought before leaving Paris. Unlike the legend, these were not sewn into the lining of a coat but merely locked up in a box which the Major broke open. Major Keller sold the stones in England to a London dealer called Mawe, thus making a lot of money. Having made his discovery, he left the carriage to his soldiers who stripped it of anything worthwhile. Realising the carriage's possible value he changed his mind and got the carriage out and had it sent back home to Düsseldorf where it arrived on 25 June! After being exhibited there for some time, the easy carriage was taken to England towards the end of 1815 by von Keller in person and handed over to His Majesty's Government for the tidy sum of £2 500. Sold again then exhibited all over the place, together with the tale of its capture drawn up by the Prussian Major, the carriage was finally bought by Mme Tussaud in 1842 for her famous London museum. It was exhibited there until it was accidentally destroyed in a fire in 1925. Only a few photographs remain today. But the tale does not stop there…
Private Collection.

Waterloo 9/8/04

Souvenir de Waterloo. — Prise de la voiture de Napoléon après la ba-
taille à Genappe le 18 Juin 1815.

DÉPOSÉ

This post card, a souvenir from Waterloo, was posted in 1904 by a French tourist visiting the battlefield.
The episode illustrated was directly inspired by the story of the capture of Napoleon's berlin, according to the version which was believed for so long. To this legend, the artist has added the fruits of his own imagination to give us his own version of the scene.
As the charging Prussian cavalry are already cutting down the teams, the Emperor, protected by a handful of soldiers, just manages to get out of the berlin. Note that although under immediate threat, he does take the time to put his frock coat on, showing in this supreme moment how phlegmatically British he could be!
Finally note that, never having been a good rider he would have had trouble throwing off his pursuers as they are too close.
Private Collection.

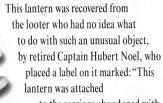

This lantern was recovered from the looter who had no idea what to do with such an unusual object, by retired Captain Hubert Noel, who placed a label on it marked: "This lantern was attached to the carriage abandoned with the teams of the French army which reached Charleroi in the night of 18-19 June 1815 during the rout after Waterloo. A grievous day, to be forever lamented". From that date on for two centuries, it has been preserved without ever leaving the spot where History turned this apparently simple object into a precious souvenir. It has been compared with the original lanterns on the photograph of the easy carriage destroyed in 1925 and it is clear that they are the same specific model.
Moreover the four examples on the landau which was captured at Quatre-Bras disappeared when it was captured. Those shown today were added later.
One can therefore conclude that this souvenir which was the pride of a collector, who was as discreet as he was cultured, comes from the landau in the Malmaison Museum.
Private Collection.

Above.
This candle was intended to be used on one of the Emperor's carriages.
The little label was put on by Hubert Noël,
no doubt the first collector of Waterloo memorabilia.
Musée Napoléon de Ligny Collection.

Left.
Emperor's easy carriage
on Avesnes'road by Maître
Eugène Leliepvre.
DR.

This other carriage was also captured, or rather found, by Major von Keller for whom 18 June must have been a glorious day indeed. This is the Emperor's landau built in 1812, also by Goeting, in which his valet, Marchand, had ridden when the headquarters was evacuated from le Caillou farm. When it reached Quatre-Bras, he had to abandon it as he could no longer make any headway. The road was jammed with fleeing troops, themselves slowed down by the cannon and wagons of all sorts which the drivers had cut free in order to get away faster. Still at the head of the pursuers, the Fusiliers of the 15th Regiment soon came across the carriage with the coat of arms and started looting it. Once again, von Keller got hold of this prize and most of its contents. It was no doubt at this moment that he had an idea – it was indeed a cunning one but it did nothing to save his honour as a Prussian officer. Two days later, the opportunist Major offered the landau and the Emperor's personal effects found in it to Marshal Blücher, explaining to his Chief-of-Staff, General von Gneisenau, how he himself had stopped the fleeing team, cutting down the drivers and just missing the Emperor in person. However it is known for certain that the Emperor, after leaving the battlefield, within a square of the 1st Grenadiers, stopped for a moment at le Caillou, then mounted a fresh horse and did not dismount until the Quatre-Bras crossroad before leaving for Charleroi. Since he rode alongside the road, across the fields, it is possible that he overtook his carriages without even seeing them as they were lost in the tumult of the rout and hidden by the failing light. This tale, taken straight from a courtesan's imagination, was taken up in the official report of the battle drawn up shortly afterwards! On the same day, Blücher wrote to his wife *"The richly embroidered ceremonial coat belonging to Napoleon together with his carriage is in our hands. It's this carriage that I am sending to you. I'm sorry that it has been damaged. Its accessories and its valuables have been looted by the troops. Its horses have disappeared. A lot of soldiers have taken loot worth five to six thousand Thalers. He [Napoleon] was riding in this carriage when he was discovered by our soldiers. He jumped out without his horse and when he got on his horse he lost his hat."*

In reality this was a spare hat found in the luggage! Moreover, if the Emperor had reached France bareheaded or wearing some form of improvised hat, the numerous witnesses to the events at the time would have mentioned the fact. Learning later that another of the Emperor's carriages was exhibited in England, the credulous Blücher still claimed that it could only be a fake! Not for an instant did the old Marshal imagine that one of his officers had duped him thus. In 1975, the landau was offered to the Malmaison Museum by Count Blücher von Walstatt, the descendant of Marshal "Vorwaert".

Copyright RMN – Daniel Arnaudet.

THE FRUIT OF ALL THIS LOOTING

Hubert Noël has already been mentioned in these pages and deserves our attention for a moment. A former captain in the Imperial army, retired in 1807, this native of Rheims settled in Charleroi where he married a certain Miss Chapel, the daughter of one of the town's notables. In 1815 he watched the arrival of the French troops and their rout four days later. Placed by fate right in the path of his sovereign, the former officer, as proof of his loyalty, started to recover the objects from Napoleon's looted carriages. He thus made up one of the first collections entirely given over to memorabilia of the Belgian Campaign. Very little remains of this campaign: a lamp, a candle, a writing case, two flasks and a few sheets of writing paper. However a document has come down to us entitled

"List of the objects found in Emperor Napoleon's carriage which was abandoned with the teams of the French army which reached Charleroi in disarray on the night of 18-19 June, a sad day to be forever lamented.

-a portable dictionary in French
-a campaign chess set
-four liquor flasks
-two oil flasks
-a "quatre valeurs" vinegar flask
-a carriage lantern
-a whole candle for the carriage
-a wax torch for use by the servants
-a stamp with the crowned 'N'
-a mould with the Imperial eagle
-a first aid packet

-a "boete" box of balance weights
-some gilt-edged sheets of paper with the effigy of the Emperor for his own use
-a little box of gold sand
-a pocket writing case made of silver with a leather sheath with a silver pen-holder
-a penknife with a spoon and fork made of vermeil decorated with silver
-a Officer of the Legion d'Honneur Cross
-a silver medal weighing three ounces showing a bust of the Emperor
-a big map of France in 1814, by military divisions
and miscellaneous other little objects."

Today the souvenir hunters would have a hard time making up this list!

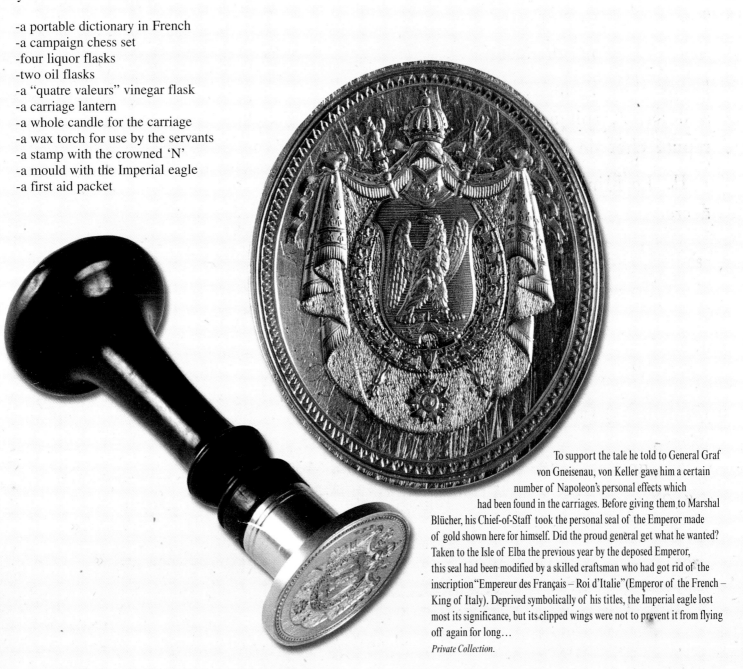

To support the tale he told to General Graf von Gneisenau, von Keller gave him a certain number of Napoleon's personal effects which had been found in the carriages. Before giving them to Marshal Blücher, his Chief-of-Staff took the personal seal of the Emperor made of gold shown here for himself. Did the proud general get what he wanted? Taken to the Isle of Elba the previous year by the deposed Emperor, this seal had been modified by a skilled craftsman who had got rid of the inscription "Empereur des Français – Roi d'Italie" (Emperor of the French – King of Italy). Deprived symbolically of his titles, the Imperial eagle lost most its significance, but its clipped wings were not to prevent it from flying off again for long…
Private Collection.

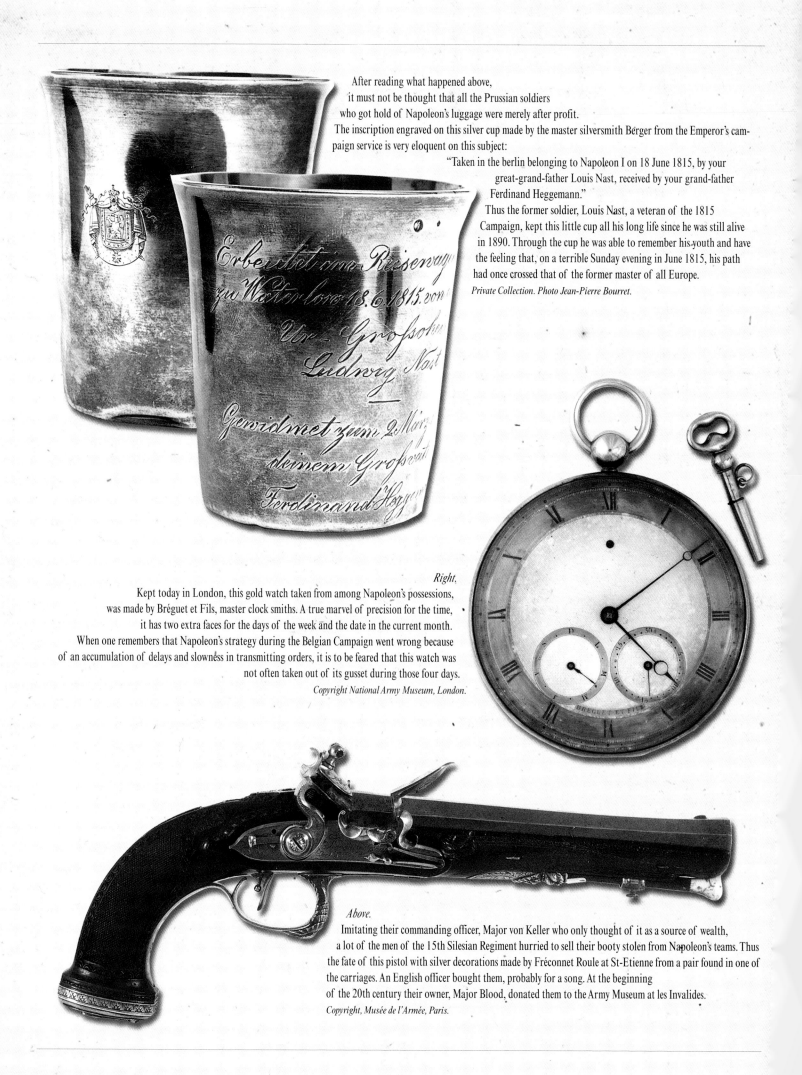

After reading what happened above,
it must not be thought that all the Prussian soldiers
who got hold of Napoleon's luggage were merely after profit.
The inscription engraved on this silver cup made by the master silversmith Berger from the Emperor's campaign service is very eloquent on this subject:

"Taken in the berlin belonging to Napoleon I on 18 June 1815, by your
great-grand-father Louis Nast, received by your grand-father
Ferdinand Heggemann."

Thus the former soldier, Louis Nast, a veteran of the 1815
Campaign, kept this little cup all his long life since he was still alive
in 1890. Through the cup he was able to remember his youth and have
the feeling that, on a terrible Sunday evening in June 1815, his path
had once crossed that of the former master of all Europe.

Private Collection. Photo Jean-Pierre Bourret.

Right,
Kept today in London, this gold watch taken from among Napoleon's possessions,
was made by Bréguet et Fils, master clock smiths. A true marvel of precision for the time,
it has two extra faces for the days of the week and the date in the current month.
When one remembers that Napoleon's strategy during the Belgian Campaign went wrong because
of an accumulation of delays and slowness in transmitting orders, it is to be feared that this watch was
not often taken out of its gusset during those four days.

Copyright National Army Museum, London.

Above.
Imitating their commanding officer, Major von Keller who only thought of it as a source of wealth,
a lot of the men of the 15th Silesian Regiment hurried to sell their booty stolen from Napoleon's teams. Thus
the fate of this pistol with silver decorations made by Fréconnet Roule at St-Etienne from a pair found in one of
the carriages. An English officer bought them, probably for a song. At the beginning
of the 20th century their owner, Major Blood, donated them to the Army Museum at les Invalides.

Copyright, Musée de l'Armée, Paris.

Because he had gone off on a campaign that nobody expected to be so brief, the Emperor's zealous servants packed his decorations. At the height of his power, when he made and unmade kings, Napoleon I had often been honoured in such a way. From these orders and medals which he hardly ever wore and which fell into the hands of the looters only two have come down to us. A silver plaque of the Order of St Joseph of Wurzburg, and the plaque of the Great Cross embroidered with gold thread of St Stephen of Hungary. On the back of the latter there is an inscription in German which says "Napoleon/18ten Juny 1815/bei der Bagage genommen" (Napoleon 18 June 1815, taken from the baggage).
Private Collection.

Left.
What was not found in the Emperor's luggage? The easy carriage comprised a book locker which contained among other things, Volume XIV of Plutarch's "Famous Men". The Prussian who got hold of this must have been more attracted by the golden eagle which decorated the front cover rather than the thoughts of the Boetian historian and moralist.
Private Collection.

This little silver writing case also comes from the collection. As was his habit, the former officer took pains to identify its origin on a fragment of parchment: "This writing case was found in Emperor Napoleon's carriage at Charleroi on 19 June 1815". It is strange to note that here again, as with the lantern, the fact that a carriage managed to reach Charleroi is mentioned, whereas it is certain that neither of the two carriages got further than Quatre-Bras. It would seem that in the days following the rout, a sort of trade in souvenirs belonging to the Emperor was set up in the town which was full of all sorts of marauders, Allied soldiers and farmers looking to do some good business. The place where these souvenirs were sold and bought seems to have occulted where they were found.

Private Collection.

Right.
Another of these objects which events transformed into the receptacle for past emotions, this little phial of "Sulfat Kinoe", taken from one of Napoleon's carriages and recovered by a chemist who put this label on it. A quite modest souvenir to evoke those terrible days which decided the fate of the whole of Europe.

Private Collection.

THE CLASHES ON 16 JUNE

On 15 June, surprised by the French Army of the North's sudden attack, the Allies did not react exactly brilliantly. The Prussians of Ziethen's 1st Corps were pushed about and hurriedly evacuated Charleroi to fall back on Fleurus. On the Brussels road, the forces entrusted to Ney advanced without meeting any resistance worth the name. At nightfall the Emperor could be pleased with himself. His plan had worked. But the following day once the turmoil had quietened down, old Blücher calculated that his three corps could be got together by mid-day. So he decided to take up a position backing on St Amand, Ligny and Sombreffe. He did not retreat any further. Nevertheless, Napoleon saw that he had an opportunity to crush the Prussian army before turning his attention to Wellington. Towards midday, the battle started. Full of enthusiasm, the men of Gérard's 4th Corps marched on St Amand, backed up by those of Vandamme's 3rd Corps whose objective was Ligny. After several hours of fierce fighting, the Ligne stream which separated the combatants started to turn red and the three burning villages seemed to come straight from hell.

But while Blücher used up all his strength counter-attacking as soon as one of his weak points was threatened, the Emperor kept a reserve of men which he used at the end of the day. Supported by Lobau's 6th Corps, the Old Guard and General Guyot's cavalry captured Ligny. Despite a desperate resistance the Prussians started to yield and their front line started to collapse. "Every one gets what he deserves", thought Napoleon, deeming Blücher out of action for some days to come and not ordering him to be pursued. At the same time at Quatre-Bras with Reille's 2nd Corps, Marshal Ney missed an opportunity with the Dutch under General Constant and the Prince of Orange. During the afternoon, the Brunswick contingent and Picton's Division came to the rescue. Despite the boldness of their attacks, Bachelu's and Foy's soldiers, supported by Piré's cavalry, soon followed by Jérôme's infantrymen and Kellerman's were not able to overcome the positions. On the Allied side, catastrophe loomed, the Duke of Brunswick was killed and the Duke of Wellington himself just escaped capture thanks to the speed of his horse.

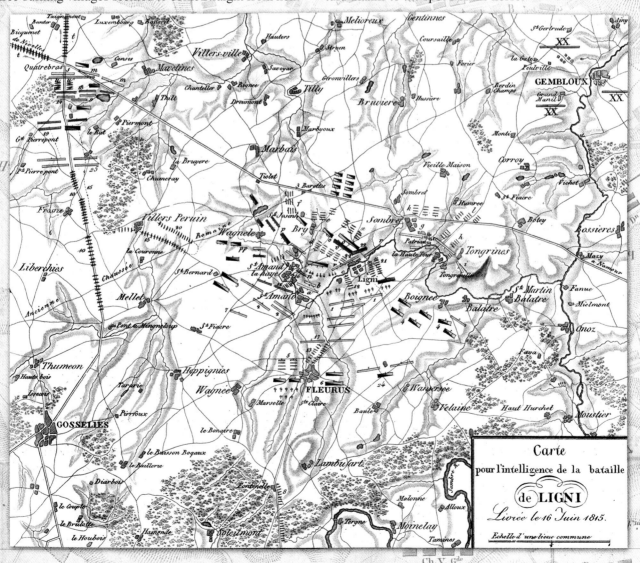

Carte pour l'intelligence de la bataille de LIGNI
Livrée le 16 Juin 1815.
Echelle d'une lieue commune

LIGNY, THE BLOODY FRAY

For the two armies facing each other, the confrontation meant something special. The Emperor's soldiers had revenge to take. It was time for the survivors of 1814, beaten a year earlier despite their staunch resistance and the bloody defeats they had inflicted on these same Prussians, to get their revenge. And what about the 1812 and 1813 prisoners who had found their country occupied after a harsh captivity? But the enemy was not to be outdone: they thought that once and for all they had beaten the oppressor of Germany and had avenged the affront at Jena. All of a sudden they had to start everything all over again. They would have to fight with renewed ardour. This hatred, forced into a paroxysm, was expressed on this 16 June 1815. On the evening of the struggle, 25 000 dead or wounded had paid their tribute.

Above.
Because they could not find an eagle, certain soldiers had to be content with breaking the royal arms off the shako plaque which was adopted after the 1814 Restoration, and getting rid of the cockerel's heads decorating the base. This plaque belonged to a Chasseur in the 12th Light who fought in the ranks of Piat's Brigade. General Girard commanded the division and was mortally wounded when the attack on La-Haye-sur-Amand which almost broke Blücher's lines failed towards 4 p.m. Having lost 25 officers and a good number of his men, among which must be counted the unfortunate owner of this ornament, the 12th Light was chased out of the village by the 6th Prussian Regiment after fierce street fighting.
Private Collection.

Below.
Ligny: the fighting at the bottom farm.
Painting after Knötel, Rights Reserved.

Above.
The Prussian army retreating by Knötel. With his chief out of danger, von Gneisenau took the very important decision to turn his march towards Wavre thus linking his line of operations into those of his allies.
Rights Reserved.

Right.
Once upon a time this shell was a danger but it did not do its job. As was often the case it had a faulty fuse and it ended its flight as a cannon ball.
Musée Napoléon de Ligny Collection.

Struggling with incredible frenzy for possession of the burning villages, the opponents, running out of ammunition, charged, butchering each other in a pitiless hand-to-hand fight. This French sabre, normally reduced to the role of campaign utensil, resumed the use for which it had been forged.
Private Collection.

Above.
These bullets and two Biscayen balls were picked up on the Ligny battlefield.
In the space of an instant after doing their horrible job, these tragic items slept beneath the soil for two centuries.
(Musée Napoléon de Ligny Collection)

Left.
An little known curiosity in the village of Sombreffe:
this cannon ball has been sealed into the cemetery wall.
Photo Gérard Lachaux, Rights Reserved.

Below.
In the holsters of the dead horse of a senior French
officer a marauder made a choice discovery:
this magnificent pair of pistols. The splendour
of these weapons, finely carved by a talented armourer,
leaves no doubt as to their value. This explains
the extreme care shown in looking after them within
the same family, generation after generation;
until the day when necessity led them to barter their
ancestor's discovery.
Private Collection.

Seven o'clock sounded on the Fleurus clock. The Emperor decided to force
the decision by piercing the enemy centre. The Reserve Cavalry Division
of the Guard under General Guyot entered Ligny from the west inexorably pushing
the Prussians who in the end gave way. This, the last "vision of victory in the Imperial
epic" as Commandant Lachouque described it was that of this unknown trooper, Dragoon
or Grenadier à Cheval, stripped of his spurs on the morrow of the battle.
Private Collection.

Napoleon at Ligny by J. Grenier.
Musée Napoléon de Ligny Collection.

Below.
A Prussian 1810-model rifle bayonet. Several battalions who were equipped with this sabre-bayonet which looked so modern were engaged in the battle. At Ligny, the precision shooting of Henckel's Tirailleurs decimated the ranks of the Imperial army which had nothing comparable to reply with. The Emperor had always thought that the courage of his soldiers armed with a bad rifle was all that was needed to tilt things in his favour. For the last time, history proved him right.
Private Collection.

THE OLD HUSSAR IN JEOPARDY

Driven by motivation which his Chief-of-Staff, General von Gneisenau, often had to calm down, Marshal Blücher had worked tirelessly all day. Counting on the support of his allies in the Army of the Netherlands under the command of Wellington, he returned blow for blow against the enemy without sparing his own troops. His line wavered when the Guards' attack broke through and his front line broke up. Beyond Ligny at the edge of the Bois du Loup, blinded by the rain which made the night all the darker, Blücher tried in vain to halt his fleeing soldiers. Suddenly noise surrounded him and his was bowled over by the charge of the 9th Cuirassiers and his horse, a magnificent white mount, a present from the Prince Regent of England was killed. But in the dark, Colonel Bigarne's troopers did not recognise Napoleon's sworn enemy. Almost fainting, he was picked up by his own men and carried aback a NCO's of Lützow Black Uhlans' horse.

Left.
Marshal Blücher rescued by his aide de camp Count von Nostiz. Engraving by Philippoteaux

Found on the battlefield, this French Cuirassier's sabre was perhaps one of those which threatened the old marshal so closely.
Musée Napoléon de Ligny Collection.

Right.
Blücher's Headquarters at Sombreffe.
Photo Gérard Lachaux, Rights reserved

Waterloo 1815.

Old Blücher at seventy-seven led the last campaign against his sworn enemies, Napoleon and the French. The defeat at Ligny did nothing to break his fierce determination which could only lead in the end to victory.

Painting by Gebauer

SILENT WITNESSES

The drummers beat out the charge, one could hear the sharp sound of the fifes and the Prussian bugles. In the crackling of the musketry, the columns advanced with heavy steps. The "Vive l'Empereur" (Long live the Emperor) was answered by the "Hurrahs" and the "Vorwaerts" (Forwards) shouted out through the explosions. Soon, dominated by the deafening bangs of the artillery, the cries of the combatants and the wounded could no longer be heard. In the heart of the burning villages, the fire roared, devouring all the shattered buildings. In the churned-up fields amidst all the noise sounded the thundering of the cavalry charges… One hundred and ninety years later, silence has returned to these now peaceful places. Only the occasional broken item recalls the turmoil of the armies at grips with each other.

View of the Ligne near Sombreffe.

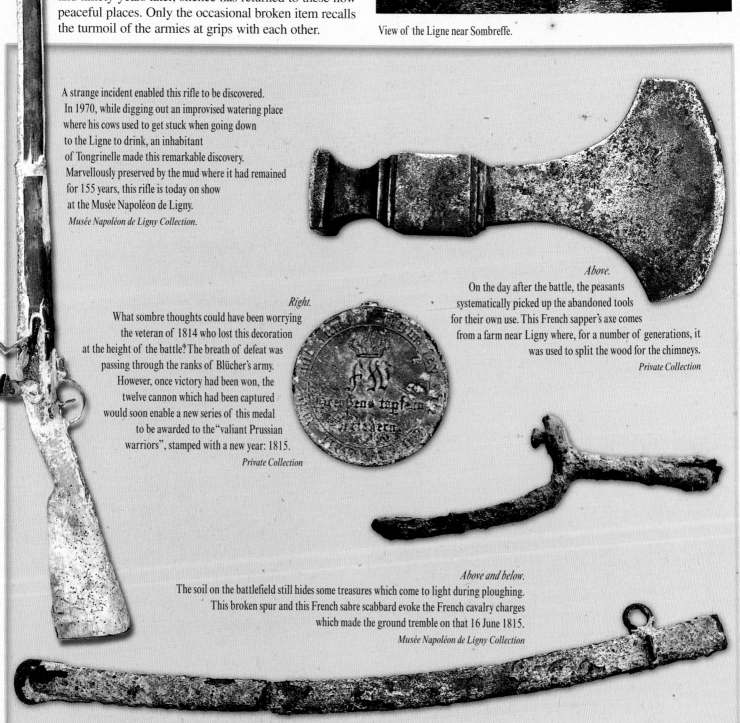

A strange incident enabled this rifle to be discovered. In 1970, while digging out an improvised watering place where his cows used to get stuck when going down to the Ligne to drink, an inhabitant of Tongrinelle made this remarkable discovery. Marvellously preserved by the mud where it had remained for 155 years, this rifle is today on show at the Musée Napoléon de Ligny.
Musée Napoléon de Ligny Collection.

Right.
What sombre thoughts could have been worrying the veteran of 1814 who lost this decoration at the height of the battle? The breath of defeat was passing through the ranks of Blücher's army. However, once victory had been won, the twelve cannon which had been captured would soon enable a new series of this medal to be awarded to the "valiant Prussian warriors", stamped with a new year: 1815.
Private Collection

Above.
On the day after the battle, the peasants systematically picked up the abandoned tools for their own use. This French sapper's axe comes from a farm near Ligny where, for a number of generations, it was used to split the wood for the chimneys.
Private Collection

Above and below.
The soil on the battlefield still hides some treasures which come to light during ploughing. This broken spur and this French sabre scabbard evoke the French cavalry charges which made the ground tremble on that 16 June 1815.
Musée Napoléon de Ligny Collection

AT THE QUATRE-BRAS CROSSROADS...

Major-General Baron Jean-Victor Constant de Rebecque had been worried for some days now. The persistent rumours indicating that a French offensive was about to start made him react despite Wellington's apparent calm. Ignoring the Duke's guidelines, the Chief-of-Staff of the Prince of Orange planned the movements he would have to carry out in the case of an attack. He placed a brigade of the Dutch Perponcher Division at Quatre-Bras whose importance had not escaped his practiced eye. On 16 June these troops delayed Ney's soldiers long enough to enable the Allied reinforcements which had been rushed up to keep hold of the crossroads of the Brussels - Charleroi and Nivelles – Namur roads. Thus Blücher's right was not threatened and Wellington, although knocked around a bit, was able to set himself up on the Mont-Saint-Jean heights. The die was cast…

Three Allied units distinguished themselves during the battle on 16 June: the 6th Dutch Hussars from the 2nd Light Cavalry Brigade under van Merlen, the 7th Belgian Battalion from the Bijlandt Brigade and the 28th North Gloucester from the Kempt Brigade. *Private Collection*

On the morning of 16 June, the staff of the 2nd Dutch Division got ready for a rough day.
Aquarelle by Hoynck van Papendrecht.
Musée Napoléon de Ligny Collection

Below.
French buttons from Reille's 2nd Corps found
on the Quatre-Bras battlefield. The 72nd and the 108th of the Line
belonged to Campi's Brigade, the 92nd and the 93rd to Gauthier's.
Private Collection

Above.
Picked up at the same place, these other buttons
whose the regimental numbers do not appear
in the order of battle of the 2nd Corps. Between the
First Restoration and the rebuilding
of the Imperial army certain regiments changed
numbers up to three times! The lovers of logic will
most certainly be forever frustrated.
Private Collection

Bayonet from an English Brown Bess rifle
found near the Quatre-Bras crossroads.
It may have belonged to one of the Highlanders
of the 42nd, so sorely tried
by Piré's Light Cavalry's charges.
Private Collection

Copied from an English
sketch of the period
by Captain Jones and
taken up by Georges
Barral in his illustrated
tour of Waterloo:
the marvellous resistance
by the English square of
the 28th North
Gloucester facing
Piré's lancers.
Private Collection

EMPIRE OR MONARCHY?

What was to be done in these troubled times? Rally the Emperor whose past mistakes were still hidden by a certain glory still preserved over and beyond his defeat? Remaining loyal to a powerless, recently-restored monarch who arrived from abroad in the enemy's baggage train? For the army and Napoleon's old soldiers the choice was not long in the making. The attraction of renewed pride, the spirit of revenge and the confused feeling of unfinished business made the decision easier. Whatever the morrow held, honour had spoken and they had to march!

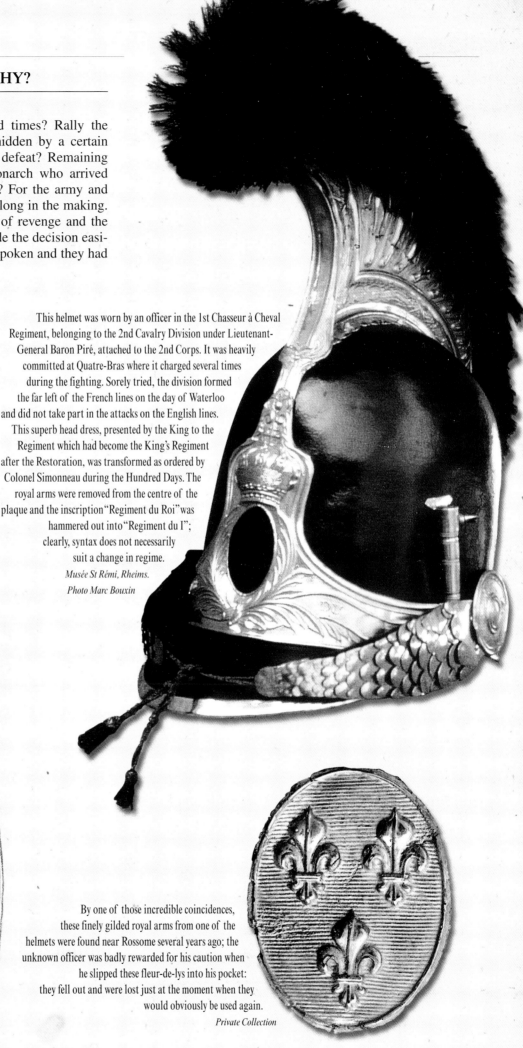

Officer in the 1st Chasseurs at Quatre-Bras.
Illustration by Gérard Lachaux, Rights Reserved

This helmet was worn by an officer in the 1st Chasseur à Cheval Regiment, belonging to the 2nd Cavalry Division under Lieutenant-General Baron Piré, attached to the 2nd Corps. It was heavily committed at Quatre-Bras where it charged several times during the fighting. Sorely tried, the division formed the far left of the French lines on the day of Waterloo and did not take part in the attacks on the English lines. This superb head dress, presented by the King to the Regiment which had become the King's Regiment after the Restoration, was transformed as ordered by Colonel Simonneau during the Hundred Days. The royal arms were removed from the centre of the plaque and the inscription "Regiment du Roi" was hammered out into "Regiment du I"; clearly, syntax does not necessarily suit a change in regime.
Musée St Rémi, Rheims.
Photo Marc Bouxin

By one of those incredible coincidences, these finely gilded royal arms from one of the helmets were found near Rossome several years ago; the unknown officer was badly rewarded for his caution when he slipped these fleur-de-lys into his pocket: they fell out and were lost just at the moment when they would obviously be used again.
Private Collection

THE SEEDS OF THOSE TERRIBLE MOMENTS

The hammering of the horseshoes on the paving stones was followed later by the roar of engines on the metalled road. Quatre-Bras or "four-ways": beyond the ditches, the land has remained the same. Of the historic crossroads nothing remains; but in the neighbouring fields time has remained suspended. The steps of the pilgrims replace those of the 1815 combatants.

When they stop with both feet in the glebe, they are making a motionless journey. The men who clashed in this place are nothing but dust now. Left behind them is a very small heritage... Between he who picks it and he who sowed it, there is no middleman... By picking at the past, you touch the hand which tightened around an invisible wish.

Above.
With his horse killed under him near the crossroads at Quatre-Bras, General Kellermann managed to get back to the French lines thanks to his presence of mind - by grabbing hold of the stirrups of two Cuirassiers from Guiton's Brigade. This acrobatic rescue enabled him, despite a sprained ankle, to lead his corps'mad charges on the Mont-Saint-Jean plateau two days later.
Painting by Victor Huen.

Left, up.
Two of these eight hollow English cannonballs were discovered recently where a battery once stood at Quatre-Bras.
Private Collection

Left, down.
Four Biscayen bullets whose origin is what is most interesting. They were respectively discovered near Gémioncourt, the farms at Lairalle and the Grand Pierrepont, and the Materne pond.
Private Collection

Left and right.
Near this famous crossroads, what remains of those furious cavalry clashes? A few small vestiges: like this broken spur, a fragment of a bridle buckle and two iron hooks swollen with rust. That's all…
Private Collection

The swan is not normally an animal associated with military heraldry. However its fine neck is to be found here on this tun stopper found near Piraumont where Picton's men faced Bachelu's troops.
Private Collection

Above.
The Gordons at Quatre-Bras.
Painting after Knötel.

Below.
Two fragments of razors, which were used in all armies and even more so in Wellington's. Indeed it was the rule, not fashion, which said that all British infantrymen should be beardless.
The difference with the opponents was heightened by their physiognomy, the clean-shaven Redcoats confronting the Gaul-like moustaches of the Imperial Army's old hands.
Private Collection

Left.
Metal, copper or iron can still survive after two centuries in spite of oxidisation. Logically the same does not apply to leather. Exceptionally, this buckle with its point has preserved the last remains of what was once a belt.
Private Collection

Below.
Debris which mean nothing to the uninitiated can suddenly crop up at his feet. This piece of bent brass was once the trigger guard of a pistol, this strangely-shaped piece of lead held the stone of a flintlock.
Private Collection

ON THE BRUSSELS ROAD

Once he learnt of the Prussians' defeat, Wellington decided to concentrate his forces on the heights of Mont-Saint-Jean. To cover this withdrawal, the French had to be held and the troops' retreat covered. The Cavalry and the Horse Artillery were mainly used for this. Cavalié Mercer, an officer in the arme savante (artillery), left a very lively account of the 17 June which he compared to a fox- hunt. Together with Lord Uxbridge, his battery just missed being caught in front of Genappes: *"All this business seemed so extravagant, so confused that for a while I could hardly believe I did not dream everything. Nevertheless, everything was very real: the General in command of the cavalry exposing himself in rearguard skirmishes and literally doing the job of a cornet! 'By God! We'll all be prisoners!' (or something like that) cried Lord Uxbridge throwing his horse at one of the garden hedges which he jumped over, leaving us to get out as best we could."*

Above.
The rocket launchers in action. Illustration by Gérard Lachaux.
Rights Reserved

Left and below.
On 16 June, Major MacDonald's rocket batteries fired twenty or so projectiles at the French troops. These rockets followed a very unsteady trajectory and did not have a great impact; this, the English artillery's avant-garde weapon, was not yet really fully operational. The head of one of these missiles has been found on the spot where they were fired from. The model presented to the Wellington Museum at Waterloo enabled this unexpected relic to be identified with certainty.
Private Collection and Musée Wellington Collection, Waterloo

Right.
The elite of the English cavalry, the Life Guards from Somerset's Brigade had the formidable honour of covering the army's retreat. Found near le Caillou farm, this sabretache plaque was probably lost on the evening of 17 June during their withdrawal.
Private Collection

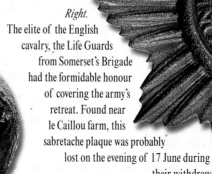

THE FRENCH JOIN BATTLE

On 18 June at about 11.30, the battle started on the left wing of the French army. The division under Prince Jérôme, Napoleon's brother, moved forward to take Hougoumont wood. Historians agree that never had an infantry attack been so badly prepared and led; the only general order given was to advance en masse and straight ahead. The enemy lying in ambush made them pay dearly to take that wood, and then at its northern edge Jérôme's unfortunate soldiers came up against the walls of a fortified farmhouse which up until then they did not know existed. Wellington had ordered it to be transformed into a fortress and it very quickly revealed itself to be impregnable despite the incredible fierceness of the French. Around this - one of the battle's high points where the three English Guards regiments distinguished them-

selves for posterity - the divisions of the 2nd Army Corps under Reille wore themselves out in a succession of assaults lasting nearly seven hours which were just as deadly as they were unsuccessful. Rarely was courage so badly repaid!

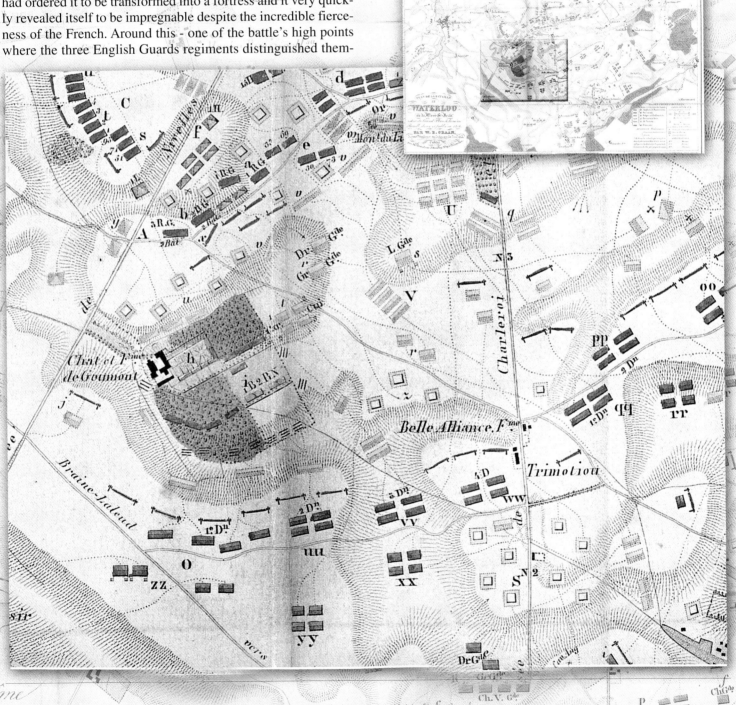

THE IRON DUKE

Just like his redoubtable opponent, Arthur Wellesley, the Duke of Wellington was born in 1769 and was considered as the most capable of all the officers in the countries fighting France. He was the only one who had not been beaten by the Emperor for the simple reason that during six years' campaigning the Duke had never faced Napoleon on the battlefield! In 1815, he was famous for his victorious leadership during the Peninsular War which ended in 1814, under the walls of Toulouse. Some months later, while travelling through Belgium, he had noticed the site at Mont-Saint-Jean and, as was his habit, he had already considered how an army could profit from it. As events led him back to the same spot after the Quatre-Bras engagement, it was all the more natural for him to choose the site for his battleground. History was about to make this general who did not like war into the person who defeated Napoleon once and for all. He was very clear-sighted with his triumph. He who was known as the Iron Duke wrote later: "*the only catastrophe which is just as bad as a lost battle is a victory.*"

Unlike Napoleon, Wellington wrote out his own orders. It was a habit of his to use one of his saddle holsters for these writing materials which indeed he used on 18 June.
Musée Wellington Collection, Waterloo

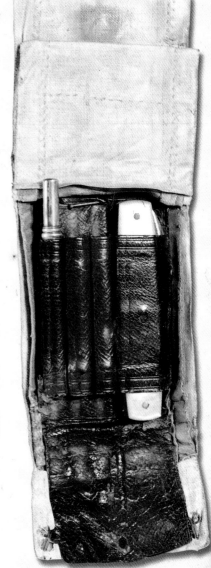

The Aspley House Museum in London carefully preserves some sheets of Wellington's notebooks. On the first shown here, the following lines penned on 17 June can be read:
"*Have your men camp near the garden where the ladders were. The cavalry will billet in the village or camp where it is.*"
Below, the Duke has crossed out this other order: "*The Prussians have a corps at St Lambert. Kindly send a patrol on your left to communicate with them. Have you sent a patrol to Braine le Chateau?*"
On the second: "*We hope to have most of the cavalry between the two big roads. This means three brigades at least between the observation brigade on the right and the Belgian cavalry and the Duke of Cumberland's Hussars. A heavy and a light brigade could remain on the left.*"
Wellington Museum Collection, London

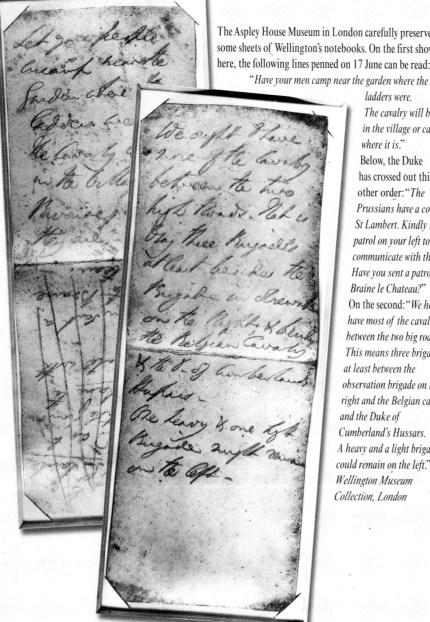

His Grace the Duke of Wellington at the time of his triumph.
Miniature after Sir Thomas Lawrence.
Private Collection

Left.

An apparently trivial article whose life has been carefully recorded. The Duke of Wellington gave his shaving mirror to Mr Palmer, warden of Strathfieldsaye Church who later bequeathed it to his grandson as a family heirloom. Then the item was auctioned on 27 August 1914 when the property was dispersed, the grandson having died without leaving any heirs. It was bought by Colonel W.P.H. Hill who in the end presented it to the National Army Museum in London on 1 December 1929.

Copyright National Army Museum, London

Above.
A general who was at home with simplicity.
In his Excellency the Duke's luggage was this
functional, rustic locker, without
any decorations.
Wellington Museum, London

Left.
The cutlery which Wellington took
on campaign. Blending luxury with
ingeniousness this beautiful silverware
enabled its owner to benefit from
the Englishman's sense of the practical
in all circumstances.
Wellington Museum Collection, London

45

A BONAPARTE
IN THE BATTLE

King of Westphalia from 1807 to 1813, Jérôme, the Emperor's youngest brother was employed as a Lieutenant-General in the Armée du Nord during the Belgian Campaign. Slightly concussed by a bullet which hit the pommel of his sword two days earlier at Quatre-Bras, the Prince led his division when it attacked on 18 June. It seems that on that day, he was more cautious since in his account of the battle drawn up a month later, he still did not know of the existence of the fortified farm at Hougoumont. Of the fight that took place in front of his eyes, he only saw the edge of a wood into which his troops kept disappearing. Although the painter gives an idealised idea of a 30-year-old general in 1815, the magic of photography reveals all the blemishes of the old man a short while before his death in 1860. Of all the officers of senior rank who took part at Waterloo he was, without doubt, together with General Reille, the one who lived longest.

Jérôme wearing the uniform of the Westpahlian Bodyguards. Painting by François-Joseph Kinsoen
Rights Reserved

Below.
A lot less famous than his older brother's, this hat was worn by Prince Jérôme on the battlefield where he was in command of the 6th Division of the 2nd Army Corps under Reille.
Musée Napoléon, château de la Pommerie

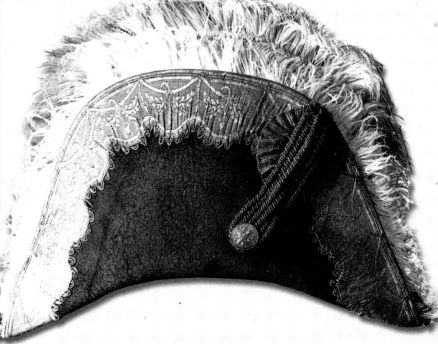

Above.
Awarded many honours by Napoleon III, his nephew the then Emperor, the man who was now called King Jérôme at the end of his life.
Cliché by Disdéri. Private Collection

COURAGE UNREWARDED

Already sorely tried during the murderous fighting at Ligny and Quatre-Bras on 16 June, the three divisions of 2nd Corps present at Waterloo had lost nothing of their enthusiasm. But they ran into the best soldiers in the English army, entrenched in a position they had had time to fortify. Without any artillery to drop direct hits on the Hougoumont buildings, their attacks ran up against the walls of the domain. Among those who went furthest, six Voltigeurs of the 1st Light succeeded in getting into the garden where of course they were wiped out.

Right.
The French attack
at Hougoumont.
Eau forte after Ernest Croft.
Musée Wellington Collection,
Waterloo

Waterloo
Entrée de la ferme d'Hougoumont

Left.
Ninety years after the battle, Hougoumont (originally "Gomont") appeared on a considerable number of postcards. This one shows the southern entrance to the farm and the end of the garden wall from which the English and the Hanoverians shot down at point blank range onto the French attackers through cleverly made crenels.
Private Collection

The gardener's house as it is today.
Photo Gérard Lachaux. Rights Reserved

"*We had the time to examine the terrain in our immediate neighbourhood. Books and papers littered the ground everywhere. The books surprised me at first but then after a closer look I understood… Each French soldier used to carry a little booklet for his pay and his effects, etc…*"Cavalié Mercer, English Artillery Officer, Waterloo Campaign diary.

"*Picked up on the field of Waterloo one month after the battle.*"This inscription penned on the cover of this French military pay book authenticates its origin. The first page of this moving souvenir gives the name of its former owner who fell at Hougoumont: Valmont, Jacques Louis from the 2nd Light Infantry Regiment, one of General Bachelu's division's many dead, sacrificed in turn after those of Jérôme and Soye.

Musée Napoléon de Ligny Collection

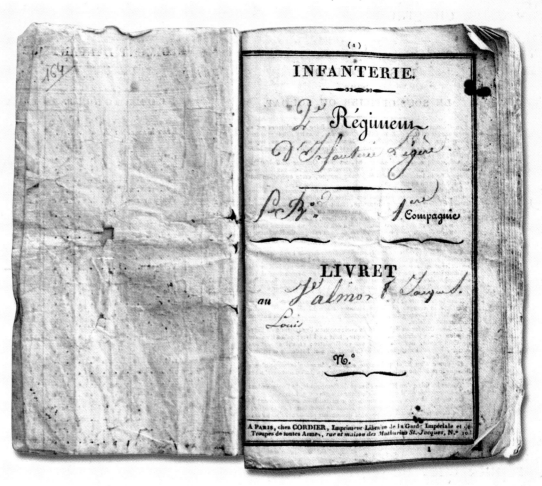

Waterloo — Hougoumont - Porte du Nord

Above.
On this post card from the beginning of the 20th century, the northern gate
still looks like it did for the combatants in 1815.
Private collection

Above.
By some miracle, this plaque from the 2nd Light of the same origin might
have belonged to the unfortunate soldier, Valmont. After the battle,
for the victors and the curious, the shako plaque was the easiest and the most
symbolic trophy to carry away. The eagles which decorated the headdresses
of the French dead most likely ended up, not in the museum collections,
but in far greater numbers on the mantelpieces and in the drawers
of anonymous households.
Musée Royal de l'Armée Collection, Brussels

Preserved in the Musée Royale de Bruxelles, this Grenadier's shako from
the 3rd Infantry Regiment has kept its 1810 cords and flounders. It was worn like that
by a soldier from General Bauduin's Brigade which was decimated in the initial attacks
on the wood. The eagle on the 1812-model plaque was presumably decapitated earlier
during Louis XVIII's first restoration.
Musée Royal de l'Armée, Brussels

Opposite page.
At the height of the fighting around Hougoumont, the epic picture of Lieutenant Legros breaking through the north door with an axe has remained in peoples'memories. But there
again, the Guards had the last word and the brave men of the 1st Light Infantry Regiment gave their lives for nothing. The "breaker-in" ("enfonceur" was his nickname) did not survive the
battle. On the original engraving, the artist strangely enough chose to show him as a simple private. After Lucien Sergent.

VANQUISHED BUT WITH HONOUR

The tragic failure of the attack on Hougoumont was the result of a lack of understanding of the battlefield and this seems to have been characteristic of all the French attacks during that day; this has not been denied by those who took part. Bought with the price of spilt blood, the resulting glory was exalted by those who were driven back from those walls. The soldiers of the last of the imperial armies never disdained the privilege of having taken part in that last battle. Two officers from the two regiments making up the 2nd Brigade of Bachelu's Division under the command of General Baron Campi have shown how true this was.

Above.
Major Guidon of the 72nd of the Line reverently kept his Légion d'Honneur and the cockade of his shako. At the same time this officer wore a decoration where the profile of Henri IV replaced that of the Emperor, and the tricolour cockade. Without any intentional ambiguity, the memory of Waterloo has brought together the two souvenirs.
Copyright, Musée de l'Armée, Paris

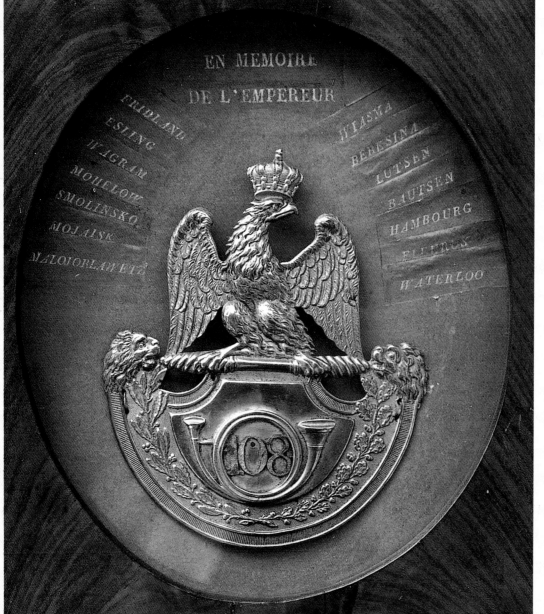

Left.
Not all the eagles fell on the battlefield. An officer of the 108th Infantry Regiment of the Line, in the same division, kept his as a souvenir of that glorious epic; even the final defeat, in golden letters, was a good reason to be proud. The hole that can be seen in the middle of the three figures shows that the plate bore another regimental number, the unfortunately unknown officer's previous posting.
Private Collection

THE GUARDS AT THEIR POST

To defend the improvised fortress intended to protect his right wing, the Duke of Wellington finally chose the men he considered to be the elite of his army. These were of course English soldiers and what's more, His Majesty's Guard, because it was true that he did not hold in high esteem the soldiers of the other countries making up his army. These would be given the task of delaying the attackers before they reached Hougoumont. In the night of 17-18 June, the men in Maitland's and Byng's Brigades worked full out to get the buildings and the domain into some form of defensive readiness. Units from four battalions made up the garrison: 1st Regiment of Foot Guards, 3rd Regiment of Foot Guards, and the famous Coldstream regiment of Foot Guards.

At a cost of more than two hundred killed and a thousand wounded, these 3 900 soldiers held off the assaults from the 12 000 Frenchmen from the 2nd Corps during the whole of the battle.

Right.
The victorious defence of Hougoumont brought glory to the three regiments of Foot Guards under Major-General George Cooke. The 1st Regiment (from which two battalions made up Maitland's brigade) left this baldric plate on the battlefield; it was already worn from use in earlier campaigns then it was deformed by remaining underground for a long time.
Copyright, Musée de l'Armée, Paris

Above.
Seconded from the Dutch army, the 1st battalion of the 2nd Nassau Regiment had the hard task of absorbing Prince Jérôme's first attack on the Hougoumont wood. Its very spirited defence was finally broken by sheer numbers. Among the objects which were found there, was naturally enough this officer's shako plaque.
Musée Royal de l'Armée Collection, Brussels.

Below.
The Goumont Gate.
Painting after a drawing by James Thiriar, from his work on Waterloo, published in 1914. *Rights Reserved*

Scribbled down right in the middle of the battle, the precision of Wellington's orders contrasts vividly with the Emperor's all too vague instructions. At a crucial moment of the defence of Hougoumont, the Guards held all his attention: *"I see that fire has spread form the haystack to the roof of the building. You must however leave your men in the parts still untouched by the fire. Be careful that no man is lost by the roof or the floor collapsing, and after they have collapsed reoccupy the ruined walls inside the garden; particularly if the enemy can get through the ruins into the house."*

Wellington Museum Collection, London

Below.

Drum used by one of the Foot Guards Battalion present at Waterloo. The shell bears George IV's number which replaced his father's, after his accession to the throne.

Copyright, National Army Museum. London

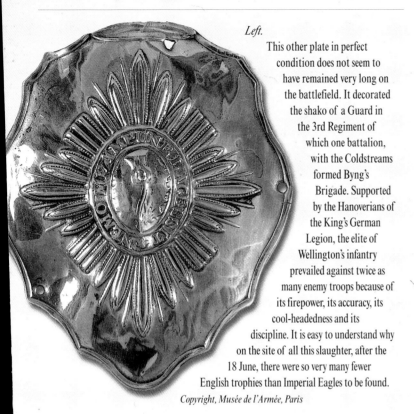

Left.

This other plate in perfect condition does not seem to have remained very long on the battlefield. It decorated the shako of a Guard in the 3rd Regiment of which one battalion, with the Coldstreams formed Byng's Brigade. Supported by the Hanoverians of the King's German Legion, the elite of Wellington's infantry prevailed against twice as many enemy troops because of its firepower, its accuracy, its cool-headedness and its discipline. It is easy to understand why on the site of all this slaughter, after the 18 June, there were so very many fewer English trophies than Imperial Eagles to be found.

Copyright, Musée de l'Armée, Paris

Above.

Shako from the Light Company of the Coldstream Regiment. It was picked up after the fighting at Hougoumont but has suffered from a prolonged stay in a humid environment. The seams were the first to go, separating the peak and the leather edging from the thick felt body. Only the metallic emblems have survived. The poor condition of this item more than likely precluded it from going to some prestigious museum collection. But its irreplaceable historical value largely makes up for that today - as far as we are concerned.

Musée Royal de l'Armée Collection, Brussels

Above.

Hougoumont burning, as Wellington probably saw it. Detail from the Waterloo Panorama.

Photo by Gérard Lachaux, Rights Reserved

THE WELL WITH A LEGEND

The legend concerning the well at Hougoumont is one of those that stick. The commentary on this post card tells the macabre anecdote for any tourist who is looking for strong sensations. *"Not far from the cart entrance to Hougoumont Farm there is a well. In order to prevent an epidemic, it was used as a mass grave immediately after the battle. According to some,* even living soldiers were flung into it because on some nights people apparently heard groans coming from the bottom of the well. It was used as a grave for 350 soldiers." When digs were carried out towards the end of the 20th century, no human bones were found there. That is how a legend starts *"people say that..."*

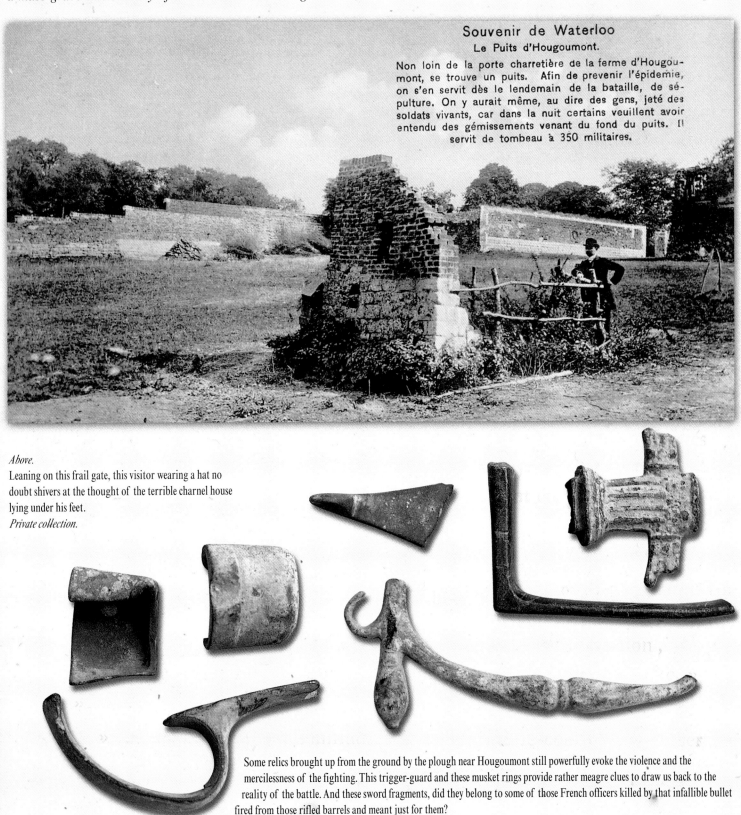

Souvenir de Waterloo
Le Puits d'Hougoumont.

Non loin de la porte charretière de la ferme d'Hougou-mont, se trouve un puits. Afin de prevenir l'épidemie, on s'en servit dès le lendemain de la bataille, de sé-pulture. On y aurait même, au dire des gens, jeté des soldats vivants, car dans la nuit certains veuillent avoir entendu des gémissements venant du fond du puits. Il servit de tombeau à 350 militaires.

Above.
Leaning on this frail gate, this visitor wearing a hat no doubt shivers at the thought of the terrible charnel house lying under his feet.
Private collection.

Some relics brought up from the ground by the plough near Hougoumont still powerfully evoke the violence and the mercilessness of the fighting. This trigger-guard and these musket rings provide rather meagre clues to draw us back to the reality of the battle. And these sword fragments, did they belong to some of those French officers killed by that infallible bullet fired from those rifled barrels and meant just for them?
Private Collection

57

DROUET D'ERLON'S ATTACK

Whereas on the left wing of the Imperial army, Reille's 2nd Corps was at grips with the Allies entrenched at Hougoumont, Drouet d'Erlon's 1st Corps preceded by an artillery barrage from the big battery of almost sixty cannon, started off in serried columns, shouting "*Long live the Emperor*". Flanked on their left by Quiot's division which was advancing parallel to the Brussels road towards La Haye-Sainte, the soldiers from the Donzelot and the Marçognet Divisions holding their weapons in the high port position marched resolutely towards the Mont-Saint-Jean plateau, towards Picton's Division drawn up in battle order. In the front line in front of the hedges along the Ohain lane, Bijland's Dutch Brigade was knocked around by the sheer mass of the French infantry. English infantry and Scots Highlanders from the Kempt and Pack Divisions resisted as best they could, and then started in turn to give ground. The outcome of the battle was suspended at this moment... Then surging forward onto Drouet d'Erlon's columns appeared Ponsonby's and Somerset's Heavy Cavalry which mowed down the French who were unable to manoeuvre and defend themselves. This whole corps which had on the attack collapsed and broke up. But the British Dragoons paid a heavy price for this decisive success. They had moved too far forward towards the big battery and were in turn charged and forced to withdraw by Jacquinot's Lancers.

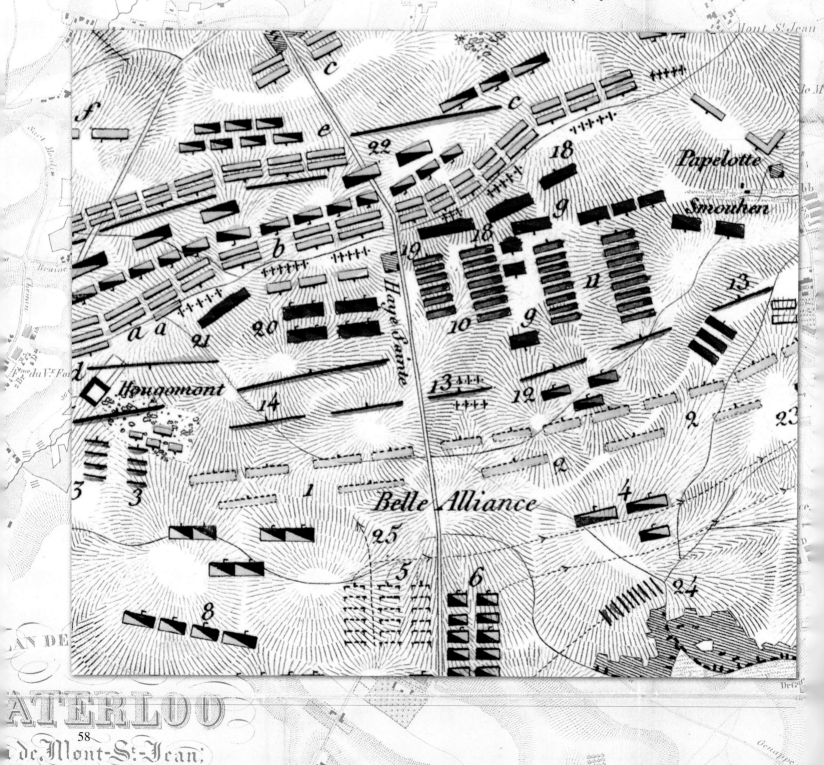

HUMAN TIDE

The 1st Corps advanced towards the Allied lines. This force of almost 10 000 men looked invincible because of its sheer might and its enthusiasm. They had not fired a single cartridge since the beginning of the campaign and were impatient to get to grips with the enemy. But their corps' very size considerably reduced its room for manoeuvre. Who ordered this Macedonian-style formation? Marshal Ney, the Comte d'Erlon, the Emperor himself? The historians are still arguing over this point. In any case, nobody had the presence of mind to remedy this situation. That was the only thing that was certain. The cannonballs cut swathes across whole columns of men marching elbow to elbow. When they joined with the opposing infantry, their attempt to deploy turned into the worst type of disorder and then, when they were charged by the cavalry, they were unable to form up into squares. The attack, carried out in this manner, was bound to fail; thus it can be said that the genie of battles was no longer on the side of the victor of Austerlitz.

The 1st Corps'attack. Drawing by Jean Augé,
Private Collection

Shako plaque belonging to a Belgian infantryman from General-Major Count van Bijlandt's Brigade stamped with the King of Holland, Willem Ist's initial. Already sorely tried at the Quatre-Bras crossroads, the unfortunate Dutch were occupying an advanced position facing Drouet d'Erlon's corps. The perfect target for the big battery, they yielded to the French attack. Their British allies unjustly reproached them for this weakness.
Copyright Musée de l'Armée, Paris

There is no possible doubt as to the fate of the owners of these buttons. Grouped in pairs, the little discs of tarnished copper bear the numbers of the Line, an accurate reminder of yesterday's campaigns and past trials for today's historians. The buttons from Quiot's Division, 54th, 55th, 28th and 105th Infantry Regiments are here in front of those of Marcognet's, the 21st, 46th, 25th and 45th. In the middle there is a button of the 6th Artillery Regiment, belonging to the corps.
Private Collection

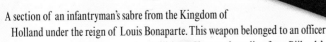

A section of an infantryman's sabre from the Kingdom of Holland under the reign of Louis Bonaparte. This weapon belonged to an officer in a Militia or Chasseur battalion from Bijlandt's Brigade.
Musée "Dernier quartier général de Napoléon" Collection

TOP HAT AND RED COATS

Among the brilliant General Staff who were present along the Allied positions that Sunday morning, was a singular character with a ruddy complexion and a gruff manner, who was listening very carefully to the Duke's instructions. Who was that civilian riding around among all the uniforms? He was no other than the commanding officer of the English 5th Infantry Division, the redoubtable Lieutenant-General Sir Thomas Picton. At the age of 56 he was tired of the war and had accepted his appointment reluctantly. A man of this calibre, one of the rare senior officers popular with his soldiers, thanked seven times by the House of Commons for his exceptional services, had still not been elevated to the dignity of Peer of the Realm. He was embittered but finally answered the call; however now, since he had arrived in Belgium, his luggage had disappeared! In a frock coat and top hat, he nevertheless took up his position without batting an eyelid. None of his soldiers wearing their red coats would have dreamt of smiling after hearing about this mishap. Even without his uniform, there was no mistaking Picton's allure; he bore his title with all the pride in his being. He shared with Ponsonby the sad privilege of being one of the two English generals killed at Waterloo. It was too much for an officer of his rank to fall on the field of honour in civilian clothes!

Above, right.
A portrait of Picton.
Private Collection

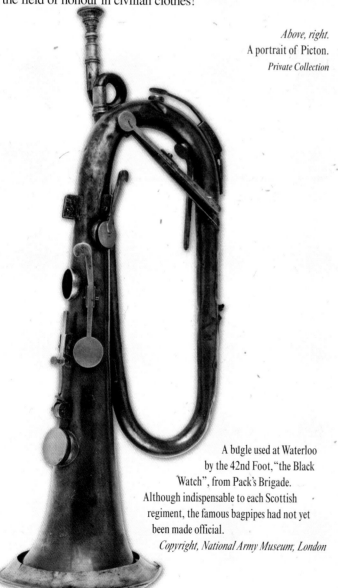

A bugle used at Waterloo by the 42nd Foot, "the Black Watch", from Pack's Brigade. Although indispensable to each Scottish regiment, the famous bagpipes had not yet been made official.
Copyright, National Army Museum, London

There are relics which are apparently without interest and which
are nevertheless among the most precious. Piously kept in the National Army
Museum in London, this bullet, misshapen by its fatal impact, is none other
than the one which killed Lieutenant-General Picton.
The valorous commander of the British 5th Division had just given the order
to Pack's Highlanders to attack the flank of a French column when he was hit
in the head by this very bullet.

Detail from the Waterloo Panorama,
Photo Gérard Lachaux. Rights Reserved

Three British uniform buttons found near the crossroads of the Brussels road and the Ohain lane. The little one, with the number 79 from the Scottish Cameron Highlanders under Lieutenant-Colonel Neil Douglas, and the one from the 42nd Royal Highland under Lieutenant-Colonel Sir Robert Macara were worn by men belonging to Picton's Division. The third comes from 40th under Major Arthur Heyland from Lambert's Brigade which was in the line behind the sand quarry.
Private Collection

The man who was carrying this coin had more luck than Sir Thomas Picton. It stopped the bullet that hit it. Who once said that a man's life was not worth a penny?
Copyright National Army Museum, London

"SCOTLAND FOREVER!"

Scotland had swayed. The 92nd was falling back pressed by the French 1st Corps. Suddenly cavalry appeared and moved up behind the Highlanders. It was three squadrons of Dragoons on their grey mounts, coming to the rescue. A patriotic shiver swept through the ranks. *"Scotland for ever!"* and six hundred men, galvanised by this rallying cry, mingling the Scots Greys' busbies with the Gordon Highlanders' yellow-striped kilts, rushed at the French. It was the enthusiasm of a nation finding itself again, of brothers-at-arms recognising each other at the height of the battle. Scotland had raised it head.

Left.
Some discoveries "speak" more than others do. This little once shiny lion's head decorated the rosette on the chin strap of a Cuirassier officer's helmet. Exalted by their success, deaf to the bugles sounding the rallying call in vain, the Scots Greys reached the foot of the "Belle Alliance" in disorder after having routed Marcognet's Division's column. Suddenly they were charged at the head and blocked by the Cuirassiers from General Travers' Brigade. At the same moment Jacquinot's Lancers took them on the flank and threw their disorganised ranks into even more confusion. In an instant, the victorious charge of Scottish Dragoons turned into a rout and they fled, trying desperately to reach their own lines. Found precisely where this clash took place, this ornament comes from the helmet of an officer from the 7th or 12th Cuirassiers who lost it in the fray.
Private Collection

 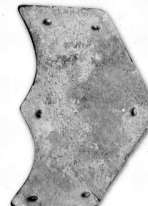

Right.
Mixed in with the small relics from the French 1st Corps found on the battlefield, these copper decorations come from the rifle shoulder-belt of a British Dragoon.
Private Collection

Coming from the battlefield, this 1796-model rifle of a Dragoon from the 6th "Inniskilling": this firearm was hooked onto the trooper's right-hand side and was probably not used during the decisive charge by Ponsonby's Division. The sabre alone could do quite enough damage.
Copyright National Army Museum, London

Right.
The 105th Infantry Regiment of the Line's Eagle captured by Captain Clark-Kennedy helped by Corporal Stiles, both from the 1st Royal Dragoons Regiment, is a historical trophy which the English still proudly keep today. Getting hold of such an emblem was no easy matter and in the evening of 18 June even after the complete defeat of the French, Wellington's army had only captured two of them. The second eagle the French lost was captured during the same action by the Scots Greys. The emblem of the 45th of the Line was captured after a very fierce struggle, by Sergeant Ewart whose glorious action made him into a national hero.
Copyright National Army Museum, London

Defending the flag. Composition by J. le Blant. *Private Collection*

SOMERSET'S BOILERMAKERS

In 1815, Major-General Lord Edward Somerset was one of the most experienced cavalry officers in the English army. He particularly distinguished himself during the Peninsular War from Talavera to Toulouse. On Wellington's request, he was given the command of the prestigious Household Cavalry Brigade. It comprised the four regiments of heavy cavalry, the 1st and 2nd Life Guards, the Royal Horse Guards and the 1st Dragoon Guards, who all vied constantly with each other for pride of first place. Only by an act of mad bravura could this rivalry be settled. The charge which was made against the Cuirassiers flanking the 1st Corps' attack was at last an opportunity to settle matters one way or another. By losing almost half their number, the King's cavalry proved beyond doubt that in fact there was no distinction to be made among them: they were all the best. Revisiting the site in 1842 a short while before his death, Lord Somerset, while evoking the sabres which hammered the helmets and the breastplates, declared to his guide who was none other than Sergeant Cotton: *"You'd have thought that they were a crowd of boilermakers at work."*

Above.
A clash between a Royal Dragoon and a Cuirassier. Detail from the Waterloo Panorama.
Photo Gérard Lachaux, Rights Reserved

Several buttons from the "Blues" have not surprisingly been found. Indeed out of a strength of 296 officers and men, 109 were killed or wounded, among them Sir Robert Hill.
Private Collection

The visor rent by a sabre blow on the helmet belonging to Lieutenant-Colonel Sir Robert Hill, commanding the Royal Regiment of Horse Guards, bears witness to the bloody clash in which the Household Brigade faced Milhaud's Cuirassiers.
Household Cavalry Museum Collection

Captain William Tyrwitt-Drake of the Royal Horse Guards, the famous "Blues", had the following inscription engraved on the guard of his sabre: *"Worn at Waterloo by Capt W T Drake, RH GDS"*.
Copyright National Army Museum

Cartridge case which belonged to Captain Kelly
of the 1st Regiment of Life Guards. As with many officers,
he had taken the trouble to replace some of his uniform accessories
with items belonging to the troopers which were better
adapted to the harsh battlefield conditions, like this cartridge
case which he nevertheless decorated with an officer's
sabretache insignia. This concern was understandable
at a time when being a captain meant charging at the head
of one's men. He was seriously wounded and was commended
by Lord Somerset in his report for the attention
of the Duke of Wellington on 24 June.
Household Cavalry Museum Collection

A Charge by the Household Cavalry Brigade.
Wellington Museum Collection, Waterloo

For the most prestigious cavalrymen of the Crown, honour demanded that they distinguish themselves in some decisive action. Thus this horse's bit and this belt attachment from the Life Guards were among the relics found at Waterloo.
Copyright Musée de l'Armée, Paris and Private Collection (Former Cotton museum)

This hoof still bearing the traces of the shoe nails belonged to Jock, the last survivor of the 2nd Life Guards' horses. A veteran of the Battle of Waterloo, this noble member of the species died in London in 1836. Proud of the glorious services he had rendered, the troopers made this hoof one of the most unexpected of relics.
Copyright National Army Museum, London

THE WRECKS ON THE EBB

Just like the sea, the wave of shakos broke against the big red dike. Like the spray, it broke into great white curls. The deadly backwash of the battle, like that of the sea, carried the human tide away. Ebbing, it left behind it its tribute of living forces like scattered pebbles, grounded wrecks of bodies and things which were no longer of any import to the swell, which reformed in the distance.

Left.
This eagle's head has known better days on a Drum-Major's chest. In his noble beak, the bird still holds a little ring which is now broken and which held a little chain linking it to a blazon located lower down on the baldric.
Private Collection

Above.
Having lost its plaque, finger guard and trigger, this broken privately-purchased pistol belonged to a French officer as did the beautifully crafted shoe buckle. These objects remind us that marching alongside their men, lieutenants and captains in the 1st Corps paid a heavy price during this disastrous engagement.
Private Collection

Right.
This musket fire-pan and stone still surrounded by its lead vice-cap come from weapons which were no doubt picked up on the morrow of the battle.
Private Collection

Left.
In the fields at Belle-Alliance, where the five brigades under Generals Bourgeois, Schmitz, Aulard, Noguès and Grenier were annihilated, the fertile ground still hides the humble relics of the great fray. These crowns once decorated the baldrics or the cartridge cases of the fallen.
Private Collection

Mont-Saint-Jean Today.
Photo Gérard Lachaux. Rights reserved

NEY'S BATTLE

On this bit of Belgian soil where Napoleon and Wellington finally faced each other, the armies straddled the Brussels-Charleroi road. On this road the farm at Haie-Sainte was the main Allied forward position. It was the key to the battlefield, according to the strategists. The first French attack by Quiot's division hardly affected the position which was staunchly defended by a battalion of the King's German legion, dug in behind its walls, making it into a second Hougoumont. The successive skirmishes on both sides, the bloody fighting around the small farm lasted for nearly five hours; Ompteda's and Kielemansegge's Hanoverians counter-attacked then were knocked about by a charge from the Cuirassiers under Milhaud, who were themselves knocked around by the Somerset Horse Guards, who in turn were shot at on their flanks by Bachelu's infantry. In the end Marshal Ney, at the head of two battalions of the Donzelot Division, got hold of the farm towards 6 p.m. Was the key to the battlefield going to open the door to victory? The English centre had given a bit and seemed to have started to pull back. But the French infantry had been decimated and was exhausted. Alone the cavalry, all of the cavalry,

tried to tilt the balance. In four epic charges, Milhaud's squadrons led Lefebvre-Desnoëttes', then Guyot's and Kellermann's after them, throwing themselves at the St-Jean plateau, against Wellington's squares. The firepower from these squares, the grapeshot from the batteries and the counter-attacks by the Allied cavalry ruined their efforts and thinned out their ranks. Although the Prince of the Moskowa personally led these desperate charges, his bold daring was no match for the course of destiny.

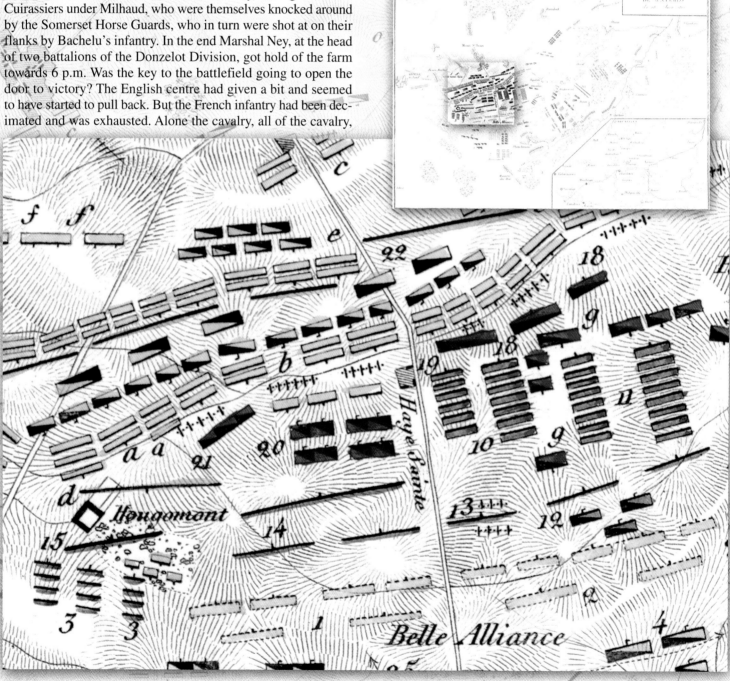

THE GERMAN FARM

Who were the Germans at La Haie-Sainte? Levied in England at the beginning of the Imperial wars, the King's German Legion consisted of former Hanoverian soldiers whose country had been invaded by France. In Spain, they had earned the privilege of being treated as equals by the English. With the return of the common foe, they prolonged their contract which was on the point of expiring, so as to be incorporated into the cosmopolitan army of the Netherlands. So, under British command, Germans were defending a Belgian farm against the French. Since 1812, things really had changed! Under his command, Wellington had soldiers from many nationalities speaking no less than seven different languages and facing him was the former master of the whole of Europe who commanded only his compatriots.

Right
Shoulder-belt plate from the 27th Foot (Enniskillen) found near the Mont-Saint-Jean crossroads. Finding such an object in the ground today is almost a major event. However, the 1st Battalion of the 27th Foot was one of the staunchest units in the English infantry. The deadly fire from the French Tirailleurs position on a hillock in front of la Haie-Sainte, put almost half the unit's strength out of action.
Private Collection

Below.
The fighting at La Haie-Sainte seen by Knötel. Once again the artist demonstrates German bravery, imagining Baring's Chasseurs attempting a sortie to no avail.

Left.
A recent, almost exceptional discovery was made near the Brussels road: this horn, intact after two centuries of oxidisation. It decorated the flap of the cartridge pouch of a Voltigeur of the Line.
Private Collection

La Haie-Sainte seen from the English lines.
Detail of the Waterloo Panorama. Photo: Gérard Lachaux. Rights Reserved.

Right.
Under Ney's leadership, the sappers from the Engineers distinguished themselves during the capture of La Haie-Sainte. These three buttons come from that legendary place. The button of the 1st Regiment marked "arme du genie-sapeurs" confirms the decisive role played by this unit on this very spot. The little one which can be qualified as a "passe-partout" button is decorated with the breastplate and the helmet, the symbol of the arm. The third one rather strangely has an anchor and is marked "genie maritime". Logic dismisses the seemingly incongruous when one remembers that the technical units were very understandably recomposed by amalgamating different units.
Private Collection

Right.
These two buttons from the King's German Legion are from Colonel Ompteda's Brigade and were found not far from la Haie-Sainte. They could come from the dark brown coat of a Hanoverian in Baring's heroic 2nd Battalion. They defended the farm with great determination, only giving it up to Ney when they had totally run out of ammunition.
Private Collection

Right.
A coat belonging to an officer in the King's German Legion, whose 5th and 8th Battalions of the Line, in position directly behind la Haie-Sainte, received the order to move forward to get Major Baring's men out. Their attempt was obstructed by a Cuirassier charge and resulted in the loss of a flag.
Copyright National Museum, London.

THE CLAHS OF FOUR THOUSAND CUIRASSIERS

The "Gros Frères" (Big Brothers) had started to charge; first those of Milhaud's 4th Corps, soon followed by the regiments from Kellermann's 3rd Corps. The tactics... What tactics? Getting this cavalry to charge excessively and blindly against infantry which had not yet been broken up? On the worst possible terrain imaginable? Victory was impossible. In a sort of absurd backwards and forwards movement, the mad succession of charges destroyed the heavy cavalry. For future generations the Cuirassiers' vain courage symbolised forever the bitter defeat at Waterloo.

Followed by his aide de camp, Ney leads the Cuirassiers from the Donop Brigade against the enemy squares. Detail from the Waterloo Panorama.
Photo Gérard Lachaux, Rights Reserved

Unlike the British, according to their regulations, the French soldiers were not provided with anything to quench their thirst. On their own initiative, they got themselves metal flasks or wickerwork-covered bottles. The traditional gourd used in Mediterranean countries was n widespread use in the Imperial armies. Emburger, the blacksmith of the 1st Squadron of the 9th Cuirassier Regiment in Farine's Brigade decorated his in a rather naïve manner with a helmet and leaves surrounding his own initials. This humble container was kept by this Waterloo survivor as a souvenir of the good moments as well as the terrible ones.
Copyright Musée de l'Armée, Paris

This helmet belongs to one of those unsung heroes, a simple Cuirassier from the 5th Regiment among the thousands whose repeated charges made the Redcoats tremble for a moment.
Private Collection, Photo Bertrand Malvaux.

Below.
The Charge of the 1st Cuirassiers.
Detail of the Waterloo Panorama.
Photo Gérard Lachaux. Rights Reserved

Following page, bottom.
Detail of the Waterloo Panorama,
Photo Gérard Lachaux. Rights Reserved

The battle over, breastplates littered the slope of Mont-Saint-Jean. They still covered the bodies of the dead and dying from the arm's twelve regiments, which they had not been able to protect from the shooting; or they were abandoned by the unhorsed troopers who had got rid of them so as to get away from the turmoil as quickly as possible. These two breastplates are among the trophies picked up by the victors who must have been surprised to have stood up to the torrent. The one on the left, a model which was brought out in 1802 went through all the Empire's wars before finally reaching Waterloo. It formerly belonged to the Cotton Collection. A corps commander who was concerned for his troopers' welfare had the busk cut off – it ended in a point, protecting the lower abdomen. This lay out was particularly uncomfortable and was modified on later models of breastplates made after 1809, like the one next to it.

Wellington Museum Collection, Waterloo. Private Collection

Above.
The Mont-Saint-Jean Farm in better days. It was located just behind the position chosen by Wellington and was never threatened by the French cavalry. However, local tradition has it that one of Milhaud's Cuirassiers managed to get through to it but was gunned down in the courtyard.

Below.
The Farm as it is today, seen from where the Allied squares were situated.

Souvenir de Waterloo
*Chemin creux où la charge des cuirassiers
de Ney brisa son élan*

WHAT SUPERB HORSEMEN!

Never was cavalry more magnificent! War became a spectacle because of the cavalry… Watch them getting nearer. At the head were the Lancers of the Guard wearing Polish style uniforms, with a shapska sporting the grooved plate, and the red kurtka with blue lapels.
Next to them came

the Dragoons with helmets surrounded by a leopard band and green coat highlighted with white. Aglets, feathers and manes flew in the wind from the charge. Wearing their bearskins which made them even bigger, the Grenadiers à Cheval advanced like a dark blue wall. Magnificent brothers of the Cuirassiers because one of the Emperor's whims, the

Carabiniers galloped heavily wearing gleaming copper armour and an ancient-style helmet surmounted by an impressive red crest. Alas, under the resplendent uniforms, man was only flesh and blood, throbbing and fragile. Shot and mud eventually stifled the magnificent energy which was spent on the slopes of Mont-Saint-Jean.

Opposite, left.
This coat called a kurtka was worn by a trooper under General Baron Edouard de Colbert, commanding the Chevau-Léger Lancers of the Guard Regiment. Unable to break the Allied infantry squares, in the end they were counter-attacked and broken by van Merlen's Light Dragoons.
Private Collection

Deprived of their leader, the courageous Colonel Letort killed on 15 June during a skirmish, the Dragoons of the Guard, led by Major Hoffmayer threw themselves at the slope of the Mont-Saint-Jean plateau. Among those who survived the shot, Captain Dulac kept the helmet he was wearing on that tragic Sunday. This sumptuous head gear bears witness to the past splendour of the Empresses Dragoons, whose epic ended in this glorious defeat.
Bourges Museum Collection deposited at the Musée de l'Armée.
Photo Bertrand Malvaux

The Charge of the Dragoon Guards.
Detail from the Waterloo Panorama.
Photo Gérard Lachaux. Rights reserved

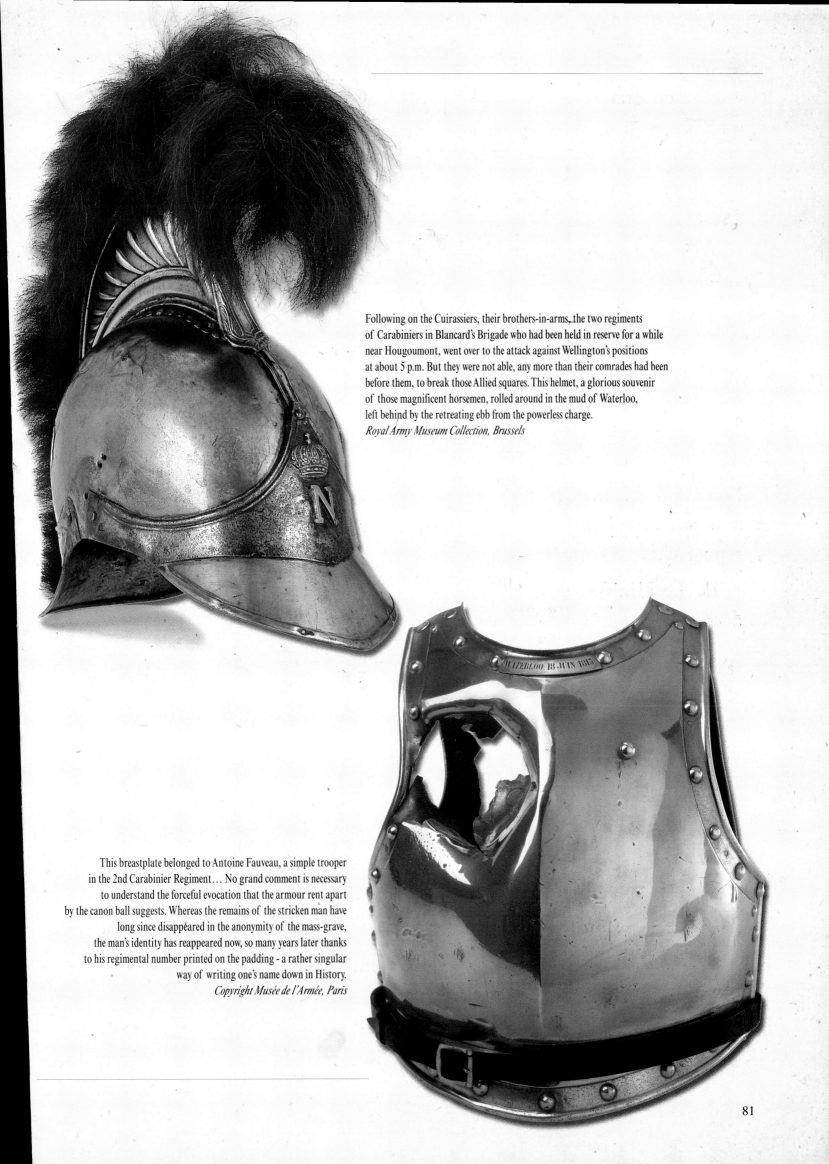

Following on the Cuirassiers, their brothers-in-arms, the two regiments of Carabiniers in Blancard's Brigade who had been held in reserve for a while near Hougoumont, went over to the attack against Wellington's positions at about 5 p.m. But they were not able, any more than their comrades had been before them, to break those Allied squares. This helmet, a glorious souvenir of those magnificent horsemen, rolled around in the mud of Waterloo, left behind by the retreating ebb from the powerless charge.
Royal Army Museum Collection, Brussels

This breastplate belonged to Antoine Fauveau, a simple trooper in the 2nd Carabinier Regiment… No grand comment is necessary to understand the forceful evocation that the armour rent apart by the canon ball suggests. Whereas the remains of the stricken man have long since disappeared in the anonymity of the mass-grave, the man's identity has reappeared now, so many years later thanks to his regimental number printed on the padding - a rather singular way of writing one's name down in History.
Copyright Musée de l'Armée, Paris

THE STRIKEN MOUNTS

They fell by the thousands without understanding anything of men's madness. Those they served threw them into the slaughter. They saw their limbs being torn off, their throats torn out, felt their guts spilling out beneath them. With all their strength they tried to advance further and yet further as they had learnt to do, but they were shot down. With madness in their eyes, they searched in vain for the man who led them, who sometimes patted them with his hand. But now only suffering answered their call. So, because they were only horses, they took a long time dying, trying to get up without understanding that it was death which had got hold of them.

*Found near le Caillou Farm:
the throat-latch crescent
of a light cavalry harness.
Who can say what high price
was paid by this, man's most
noble conquest?*
Private Collection

Above.
*These two hearts, broken
by canister, decorated the breast
of horses cut down in full charge
by the English artillery.*
Private Collection

Dragoon's Horse.
Detail of the Waterloo Panorama,
Photo Gérard Lachaux, Rights Reserved

This finely worked throat-latch
crescent and belt buckle for a cavalry
sabre give an idea of how magnificent
officers' cavalry equipment was.
Finery was as normal on parade
as it was on the battlefield.
Private Collections

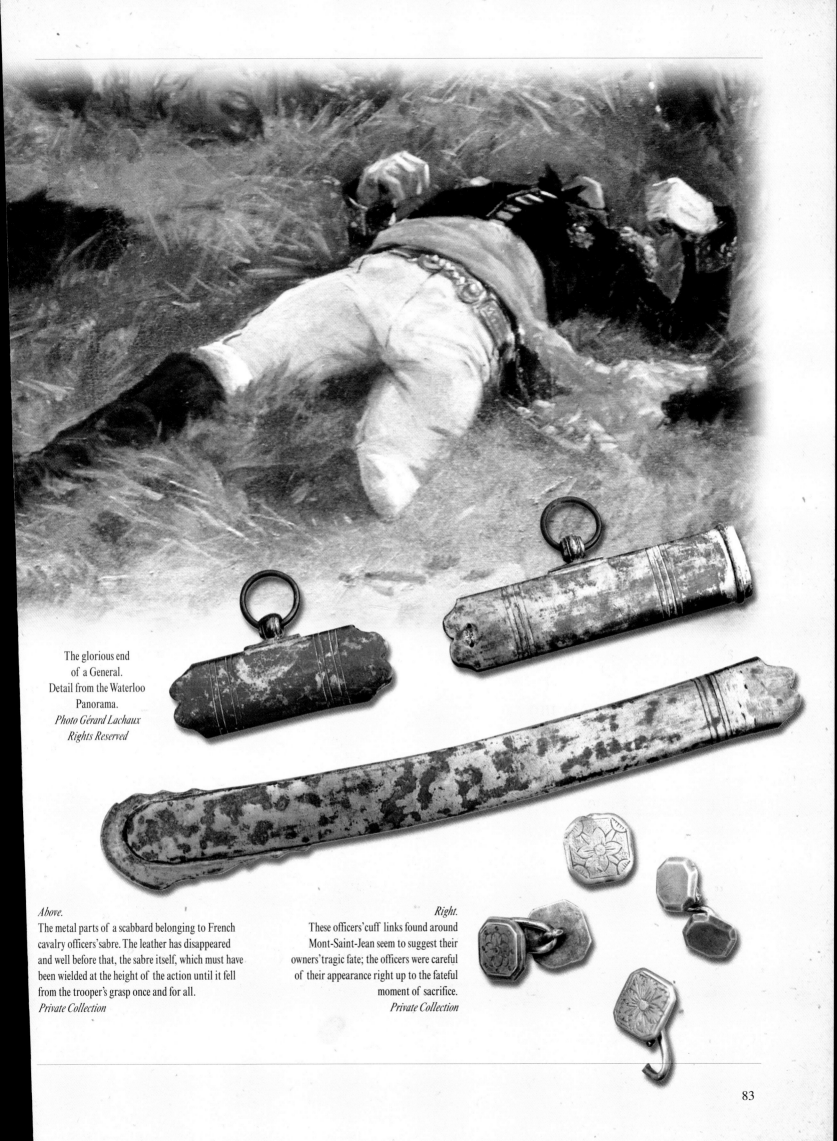

The glorious end
of a General.
Detail from the Waterloo
Panorama.
Photo Gérard Lachaux
Rights Reserved

Above.
The metal parts of a scabbard belonging to French
cavalry officers' sabre. The leather has disappeared
and well before that, the sabre itself, which must have
been wielded at the height of the action until it fell
from the trooper's grasp once and for all.
Private Collection

Right.
These officers' cuff links found around
Mont-Saint-Jean seem to suggest their
owners' tragic fate; the officers were careful
of their appearance right up to the fateful
moment of sacrifice.
Private Collection

WELLINGTON'S SQUARES

The Duke said that they were the "*dregs of society*" yet he had complete faith in them. Enrolled for seven years or for life, His Gracious Majesty's soldiers lived and died under iron discipline. The lash was the only reward if they even thought of addressing an officer without being invited to do so. Theft and the slightest refusal to obey were punishable by death. If the god of battles spared them they could hope to become NCOs. For them, there would never be any hope of obtaining promotion. When the time came to retire, if no feat of arms had ensured a meagre pension for them, they were reduced to begging for bread. For this, those who were mutilated could take advantage of their wounds. In fact, these men had no hope outside the army, no other family but their battalion, no other life but marching and fighting. They had become warriors, cowing in front of their masters and throwing out their chests in front of the enemy. Wellington had not got it wrong!

Below.
A broken weapon like so many hundreds found on the evening of 18 June…
This English Brown Bess rifle was picked up as it was in 1815.
Musée "Dernier quartier général de Napoléon" Collection

Below.
A square of Scots.
Detail from the Waterloo Panorama,
Photo Gérard Lachaux, Rights Reserved

Left.
The parts of the Brown Bess
rifle which held the ramrod
which was
indispensable for
re-loading.
Private Collection

Left.
Come hell or high
water, the English
squares held.
The Guards and the
Highlanders, of which some buttons have been
found, were the staunchest elements.
Private Collection

Right.
An English oboe which should have
played the victorious *"God save the King"*.
The fate of Wellington's musician,
who carried the instrument dismantled
in his bag, decided otherwise.
Copyright Musée de l'Armée, Paris

Left.
Wellington owed his victory to his artillerymen's cool-headedness. Abandoning their guns and seeking refuge within the infantry squares, then going back hardily to their posts after each of the charges had finished, they contributed considerably to the bloody failure of the French cavalry. Some buttons belonging to these courageous servers were found where the indomitable cannon were lined up.

The inscription "Royal Regiment of Artillery" was to be found on the mounted artillerymen's dolmans. Three superimposed cannon decorated those of the Foot Artillery.
Private Collection

Regulation English pistol, the model adopted in 1796. It has reached us after being in Sergeant Cotton's equipment. Was this weapon lost in such dramatic circumstances?
Musée Napolóen de Ligny Collection (Former Cotton Museum)

Below.
Artillerymen in great danger.
Detail from the Waterloo Panorama,
Photo Gérard Lachaux, Rights Reserved

87

SEVERAL MASTERS,
ONLY ONE DESTINY

Chance and history sometimes beget strange destinies. In 1815, General Major van Merlen commanded the 2nd Light Cavalry Brigade of the Dutch-Belgian Division under Lieutenant-General Baron de Collaërt. However, the previous year, he was still serving in the ranks of the Red Lancers of the Imperial Guard.

At Waterloo he had to fight against his erstwhile comrades. He was prey to dark foreboding. He wrote to his wife on the eve of the fight to say good-bye. His premonition of death turned out to be correct. Hit by a cannonball he died on the battlefield where his body was never found.

Above.
General van Merlen at Waterloo. The scene shows precisely what was witnessed and written down by Major Edward Nevil MacCready, who was serving in 1815 as an ensign in the ranks of the 2nd battalion of the 30th Foot. "*After the battle began, I was taking some refreshments with him and General de Ghigny, commanding the 1st Light Cavalry Brigade, who remarked that the enemy artillery fire was getting more intense. 'Yes', said General van Merlen, 'we are going to have a hot day and for me, it'll be my last!' 'Don't say that, my dear friend', retorted General Ghigny, 'Please God, you'll see a good many more.' 'Never', said van Merlen sadly, 'I'll never see another!'*"
Painting after a drawing by James Thiriar, taken from his work on Waterloo, published in 1914. Rights Reserved

Far from disowning his past in the service of the Emperor, the General kept this telescope decorated with the Eagle of his former master and wore his Légion d'Honneur right to the end, even among his new allies.
Musée de l'Armée Collection, Paris

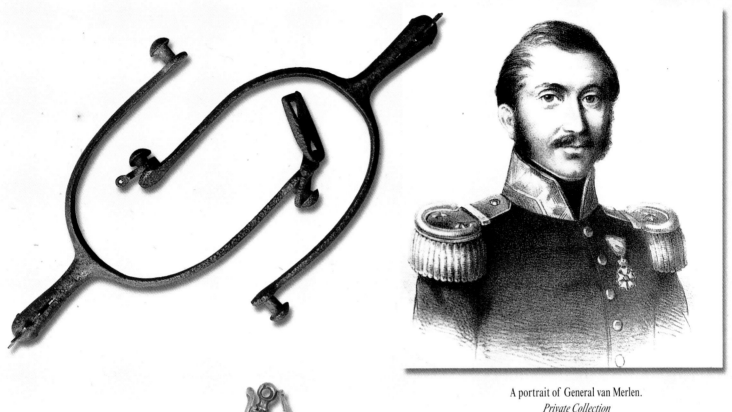

A portrait of General van Merlen.
Private Collection

Above.
It is impossible to tell which brigade these Dutch pistol and spurs come from: either
the van Zoutlande Carabinier Brigade or the Light Cavalry under Ghigny and van Merlen.
Royal Army Museum Collection, Brussels

de Heeren Officieren van het Regement Hussaren №6
in dienste van
Zijne Majesteit den koning der Nederlanden!
Aangevoerd door den Colonel Boreel, Ridder der Militaire Willems-Orde 3ᵉ Classe;
Aan hunne brave Wapenbroeders, gesneuveld op den 18 Junij 1815 bij de bataille van Waterloo.

GENERAAL MAJOOR van MERLEN.
COMMANDEERENDE DE BRIGADE LIGTE CAVALLERIE.
RITMEESTER WILLEM van WŸNBERGEN.
IDEM MAURITZ van HEŸDEN.
LUITENANT WILLEM VERHELLOUW.
IDEM WILLEM WOLFF.
JONKER CORNELIS BREDA.

Hun, die voor het Vaderland, in 't harnas zijn gestorven
Is door dien heldendaad Onsterflijke Eer verworven.

Left.
As if outside time, in the contemplative quiet
of the church at Waterloo his name appears
on one of the commemorative marble plaques
for those who fell on 18 June.
Photo Gérard Lachaux, Rights Reserved

THE PRUSSIANS ARE COMMING

On the right wing of the Imperial army, General Durutte's 4th Division arrived just in time to take part in Drouet d'Erlon's big attack whose failure it shared, although to a lesser degree. Caught up with Best's and Wicke's Hanoverians, Durutte's division had to move back under the onslaught of Vandeleur's Light Cavalry charges. Towards 3 p.m., the 4th Division advanced again, preceded by some tirailleurs. It went off at an angle towards la Papelotte farm to counter the Nassau Brigade under the Prince of Saxe-Weimar. A succession of confused engagements whose only object was to hold the line soaked the approaches to la Papelotte farm, Smohain Village and the Chateau of Frichemont with blood until seven in the evening; Napoleon however was looking for a breakthrough towards Mont-Saint-Jean. Coming out of the Paris woods where they had gathered, Blücher's Prussians - which until then were thought to be out of action ever since Ligny -entered the battle. Lobau's corps, supporting Durutte's, resisted but was overrun by Bülow's up to the village of Plancenoit, threatening the whole of the Imperial army's retreat. Inevitably, the Prussians' crushing numerical superiority carried everything with it... Napoleon opposed them with the Young Guard under Duhesme

who in turn yielded... Two battalions of the Old Guard stabilised the front, chased Bülow's infantry out of Plancenoit which was devastated by this fight to the bitter end. This was the last respite for the Emperor who relied on risking his all against Wellington with the elite of his army. But behind Bülow's corps there was Pirch's, and at la Papelotte, Durutte's soldiers were under attack from all of Ziethen's corps... The desperate situation nevertheless stimulated a last and formidable burst of endeavour from the Eagle.

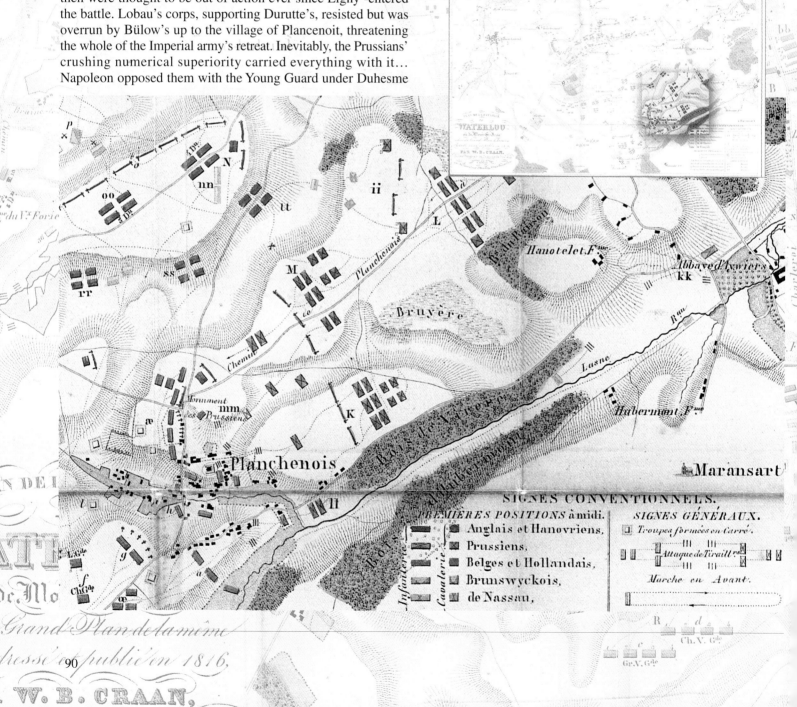

FIGHT AT LA PAPELOTTE – IN VAIN

Were the infantrymen of the 4th Division unworthy? Did the Nassau troops under Prince Bernhard of Saxe-Weimar break up? History has not done justice to yesterday's enemies. The Emperor himself denigrated Durutte's soldiers, accusing them of reprehensible weakness: "*It was there that one was supposed to have heard the cry* 'Run for your lives'". The German's account of his own men was no better: "they fled and I got them to rally a quarter of an hour from the battlefield". With anger that only their respect for him tempered, his officers denied this vigorously. Far away from the decisive fighting taking place on the slopes of Mont-Saint-Jean and the hillocks of Plancenoit, the two sides fought a bitter duel on their little bit of ground for hours on end. Although in their hundreds, their dead were not numerous enough to be part of the legend.

Above.
View of Papelotte.
Reserved rights

Right.
This bucolic view of the Papelotte farm gives no hint of the violence of the fighting which took place between Durutte's soldiers and those of the Prince of Saxe-Weimar, for possession of this part of the battlefield. *Private Collection*

Shako belonging to an officer from the 95th of the Line who took part in the fighting. While all about them was collapsing the regiment's survivors retreated in good order around their Eagle. It was this unit that Ney harangued desperately: "*Come and see how a Maréchal of France dies!*" The officer's headdress has come down to us intact whereas the famous quotation has been lost to the winds of history and legend. *Musée Royal Belge Collection, Brussels*

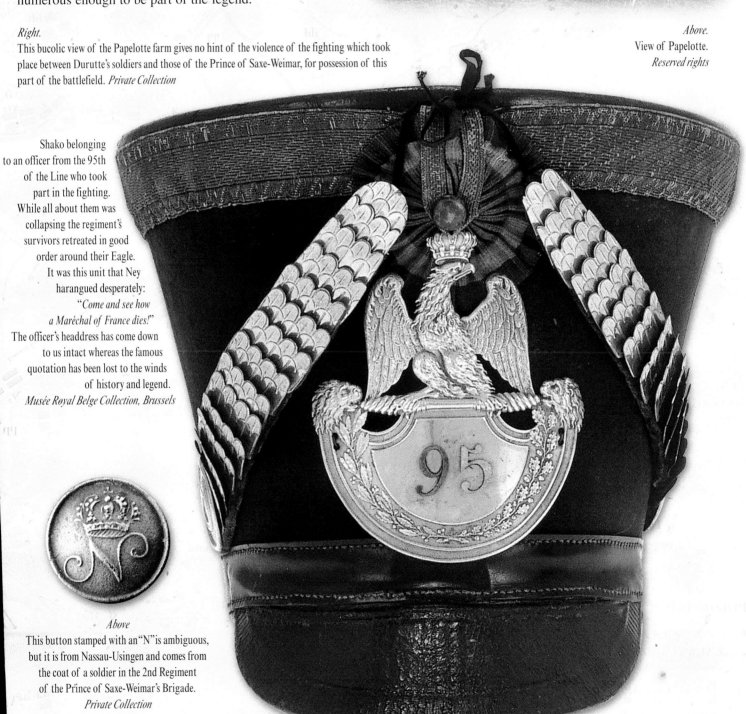

Above
This button stamped with an "N" is ambiguous, but it is from Nassau-Usingen and comes from the coat of a soldier in the 2nd Regiment of the Prince of Saxe-Weimar's Brigade. *Private Collection*

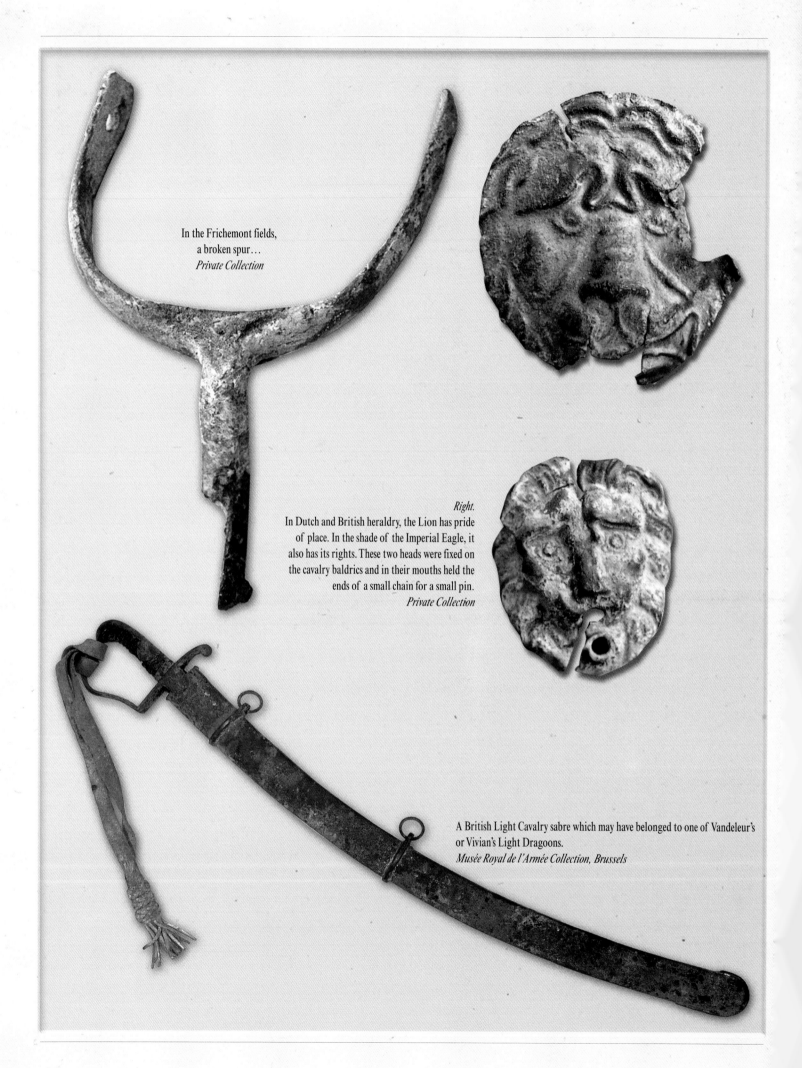

In the Frichemont fields,
a broken spur…
Private Collection

Right.
In Dutch and British heraldry, the Lion has pride
of place. In the shade of the Imperial Eagle, it
also has its rights. These two heads were fixed on
the cavalry baldrics and in their mouths held the
ends of a small chain for a small pin.
Private Collection

A British Light Cavalry sabre which may have belonged to one of Vandeleur's
or Vivian's Light Dragoons.
Musée Royal de l'Armée Collection, Brussels

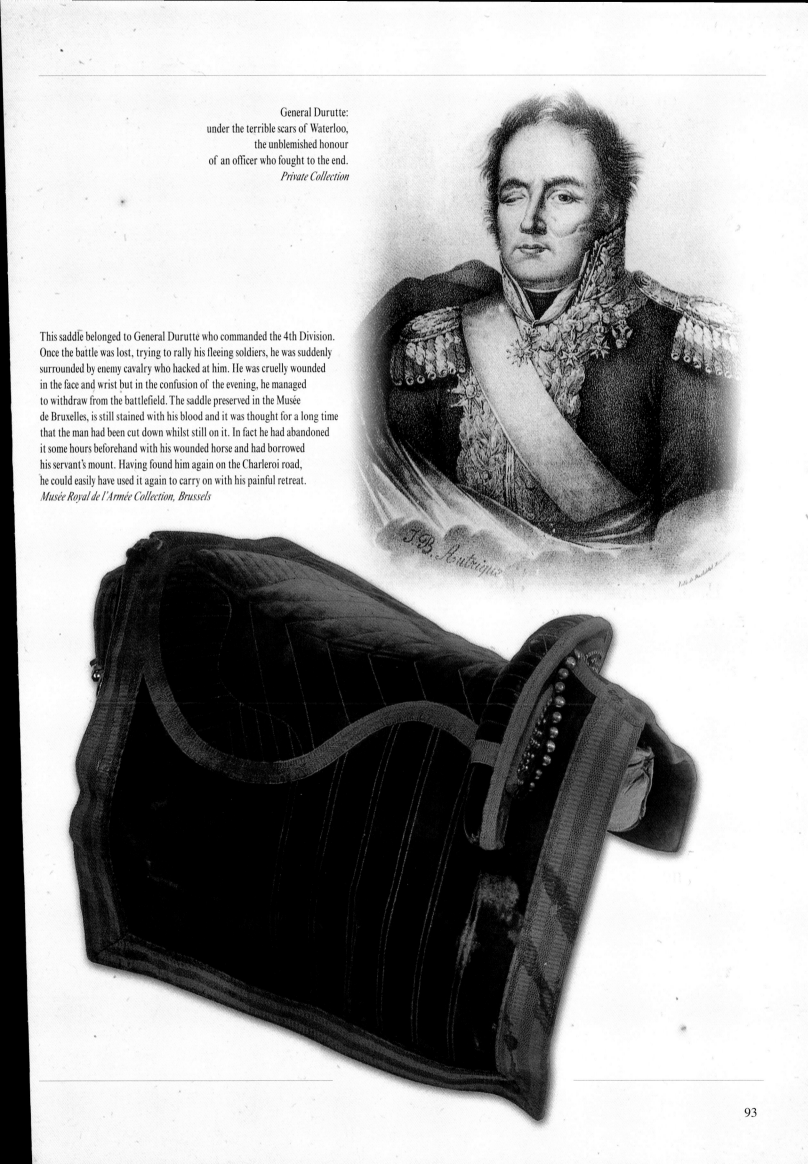

General Durutte:
under the terrible scars of Waterloo,
the unblemished honour
of an officer who fought to the end.
Private Collection

This saddle belonged to General Durutte who commanded the 4th Division. Once the battle was lost, trying to rally his fleeing soldiers, he was suddenly surrounded by enemy cavalry who hacked at him. He was cruelly wounded in the face and wrist but in the confusion of the evening, he managed to withdraw from the battlefield. The saddle preserved in the Musée de Bruxelles, is still stained with his blood and it was thought for a long time that the man had been cut down whilst still on it. In fact he had abandoned it some hours beforehand with his wounded horse and had borrowed his servant's mount. Having found him again on the Charleroi road, he could easily have used it again to carry on with his painful retreat.
Musée Royal de l'Armée Collection, Brussels

"THEY GOT US TO MANOEUVRE LIKE PUMPKINS"

"Laon, 26 June 1815.

I can't believe we were defeated! They got us to manoeuvre around like pumpkins. With my regiment I was a flanker on the right of the army for almost the whole of the battle. We were told that Marshal Grouchy was going to come to the spot which was only guarded by my regiment, three cannon and a battalion of light infantry. Only instead of Marshal Grouchy it was Blücher's corps which turned up. You can imagine how that sorted us out! We were driven in and the enemy was on our tails in an instant." The man who wrote these indignant lines was Colonel Marcellin de Marbot, commanding the 7th Hussars. Ordered to scout out the French army's right, it was only later that he discovered Bülow's Prussian corps approaching. A prey to a strange form of inertia, the famous memoir writer did not order any reconnaissance worthy of the name in the direction of Lasnes and Saint Lambert. Fifteen years later, he did not hesitate to re-write the story and given himself a more flattering role.

Shako and pelisse worn at Waterloo by Colonel de Marbot.
Copyright, Musée de l'Armée, Paris

Portrait of Colonel de Marbot, wearing a Chasseur uniform.
Private Collection

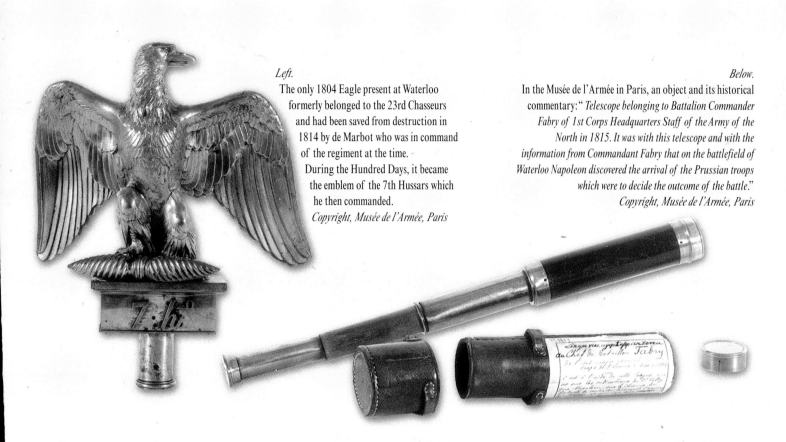

Left.
The only 1804 Eagle present at Waterloo formerly belonged to the 23rd Chasseurs and had been saved from destruction in 1814 by de Marbot who was in command of the regiment at the time. During the Hundred Days, it became the emblem of the 7th Hussars which he then commanded.
Copyright, Musée de l'Armée, Paris

Below.
In the Musée de l'Armée in Paris, an object and its historical commentary: " *Telescope belonging to Battalion Commander Fabry of 1st Corps Headquarters Staff of the Army of the North in 1815. It was with this telescope and with the information from Commandant Fabry that on the battlefield of Waterloo Napoleon discovered the arrival of the Prussian troops which were to decide the outcome of the battle.*"
Copyright, Musée de l'Armée, Paris

Scouts from the 7th Hussars. Painting after a drawing by James Thiriar, taken from his work on Waterloo, published in 1914.
Rights Reserved

THE YOUNG GUARD'S FATE

When he reclaimed the throne, the Emperor resurrected the Young Guard. Voltigeurs and tirailleurs - the hydra whose heads he had multiplied in 1813 to contain the collapse of his empire, was reformed in great haste. Deprived of two regiments, hurried to Vendée which was rebelling, only eight of the Young Guard's battalions lined up along the road to Brussels and were present at the battle, holding their fire for the whole of the morning. Their hour was to come… When the dreadful danger could no longer be ignored the Emperor gave them a sacrificial mission. Facing Bülow's 30 000 Prussians, they had to hold no matter what the cost and defend the army which was being exposed to a fatal blow. There were only 4 000 of them and they went down. Let the bells of Plancenoit toll the knell. Salute the memory of Duhesme's soldiers, this time there was no miracle, the Young Guard had died, definitively.

C.Röchling.

An Eagle of the Young Guard with a label which one would want to see more often. The headdress belonged to a soldier in Duhesme's Division. The anonymous writer has penned the emotion his discovery caused him for posterity.
Private Collection

Plancenoit's belfry.
Photo Gérard Lachaux, Rights Reserved

Opposite, left.
In the burning village of Plancenoit, the 2nd Pomeranian Infantry Regiment successfully charged the Chasseurs of the Old Guard who had come to the rescue. Forgetting that daylight was failing Röchling, the painter, glorified his compatriots' valour in his picture.

The commanding officer of the Young Guard himself was killed. Mortally wounded between Plancenoit and Rossomme, General Duhesme breathed his last, two days after the battle, in the Roi d'Espagne tavern in Genappe in spite of being looked after by Surgeon Brieske, from Blücher's headquarters. The buckle from his belt which can be seen in the Waterloo showcase at the Musée de l'Armée in Paris, and his monument which still stands in front of the austere brick wall of Ways church recall his glorious end. The only known portrait of him shows him as a young general at the beginning of the Empire.

Copyright Musée de l'Armée, Paris

Below.
Positioned at right angles at the tip of the battle lines, Lobau's 6th Corps with scarcely 10 000 men, successfully resisted the arrival of the 25 000 men of Bülow's 4th Corps. As if for a last inspection for those who disappeared, the presence of regiments from Lieutenant-General Baron Simmer's division is revealed by the buttons which have been found.

Private Collection

A FUSILIER CALLED VADUREL

"I fell in the high rye. I fell near a village whose name I do not know. The twilight of the charnel-house enveloped my death throes. There is nothing left of me… Conscripted in Picardy, I left Amiens and my mother. 1813! The German Campaign, what trials! After a lot of marching and fighting, I was made a prisoner. In 1814, the Emperor left for exile. I was allowed to return home. But the army had not finished with me. A re-recruited deserter! That was my status. In February 1815 having donned my shako, I waited to do my time. I was almost 24. I was a simple fusilier in the 47th. That's all I know. What happened to me? I lost my memory in a blast of shot. Near my corpse which the looters had already searched, an unknown person picked up a little booklet whose pages were turning in the wind. Memory of me hangs only by these yellowed pages. Who will know how to read between the lines? A vulgar trophy for some, a derisory enigma for a few others who will insist that my regiment was not even there!

Forget the battle and the drums for a moment! Forget the soldier and the uniform! Think only of the poor man whose life was stolen… One poor man among twenty thousand others…"

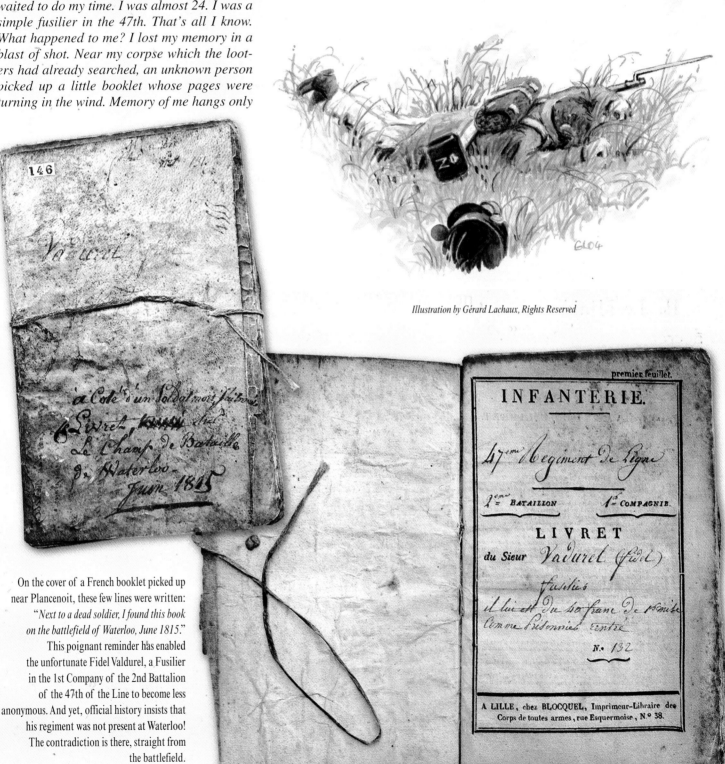

Illustration by Gérard Lachaux, Rights Reserved

On the cover of a French booklet picked up near Plancenoit, these few lines were written: *"Next to a dead soldier, I found this book on the battlefield of Waterloo, June 1815."*
This poignant reminder has enabled the unfortunate Fidel Valdurel, a Fusilier in the 1st Company of the 2nd Battalion of the 47th of the Line to become less anonymous. And yet, official history insists that his regiment was not present at Waterloo! The contradiction is there, straight from the battlefield.
Private Collection

WHERE IS GROUCHY?

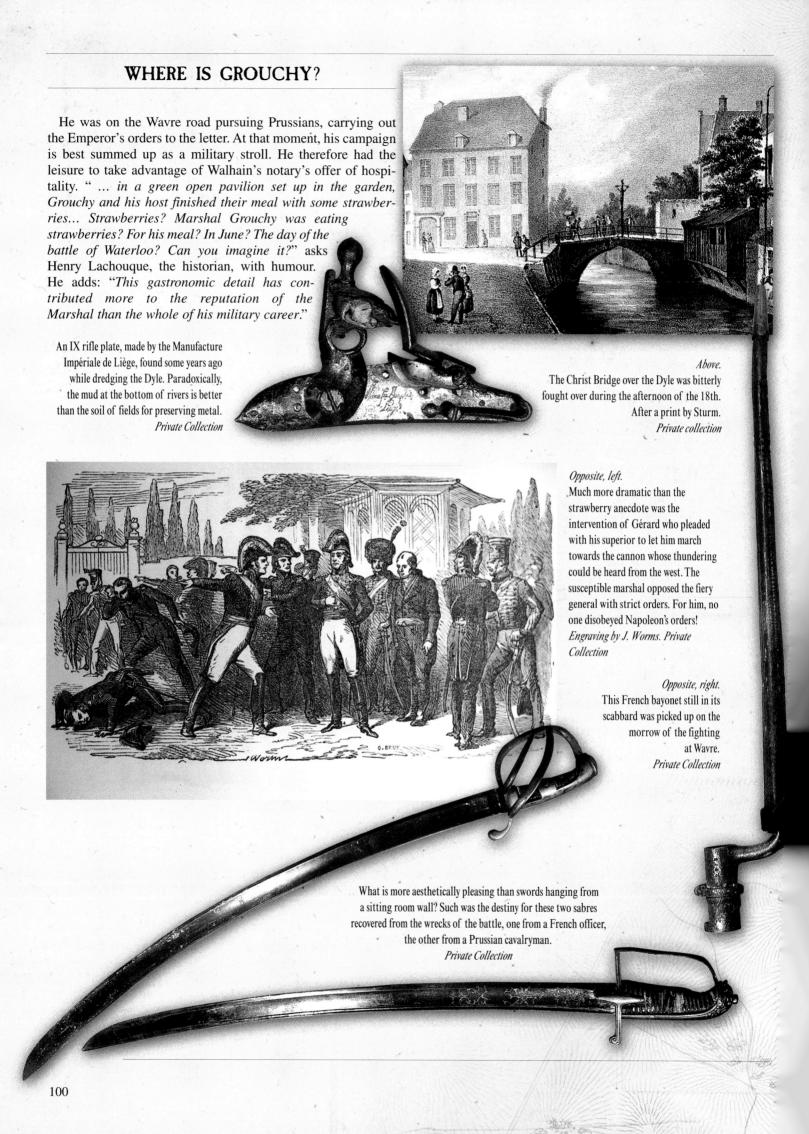

He was on the Wavre road pursuing Prussians, carrying out the Emperor's orders to the letter. At that moment, his campaign is best summed up as a military stroll. He therefore had the leisure to take advantage of Walhain's notary's offer of hospitality. " ... *in a green open pavilion set up in the garden, Grouchy and his host finished their meal with some strawberries... Strawberries? Marshal Grouchy was eating strawberries? For his meal? In June? The day of the battle of Waterloo? Can you imagine it?*" asks Henry Lachouque, the historian, with humour. He adds: "*This gastronomic detail has contributed more to the reputation of the Marshal than the whole of his military career.*"

An IX rifle plate, made by the Manufacture Impériale de Liège, found some years ago while dredging the Dyle. Paradoxically, the mud at the bottom of rivers is better than the soil of fields for preserving metal.
Private Collection

Above.
The Christ Bridge over the Dyle was bitterly fought over during the afternoon of the 18th.
After a print by Sturm.
Private collection

Opposite, left.
Much more dramatic than the strawberry anecdote was the intervention of Gérard who pleaded with his superior to let him march towards the cannon whose thundering could be heard from the west. The susceptible marshal opposed the fiery general with strict orders. For him, no one disobeyed Napoleon's orders!
Engraving by J. Worms. Private Collection

Opposite, right.
This French bayonet still in its scabbard was picked up on the morrow of the fighting at Wavre.
Private Collection

What is more aesthetically pleasing than swords hanging from a sitting room wall? Such was the destiny for these two sabres recovered from the wrecks of the battle, one from a French officer, the other from a Prussian cavalryman.
Private Collection

THE FATAL OUTCOME

The Imperial Army was at bay, under pressure on its right from the Prussians and terribly weakened by its fruitless attacks on the Mont-Saint-Jean plateau. But Napoleon would not admit defeat. Gambling everything and changing the course of destiny with a last daring stroke was in his blood. In the evening towards the end of indecisive battles he had often snatched victory by some bold, final effort. He had his Guard left and nothing had ever resisted his "Grognards" of Eylau and Montmirail… At 8 p.m. it was dusk when Morand's and Friand's Chasseurs and Grenadiers, drawing with them the survivors from Erlon's and Reille's corps reached the Mont-Saint-Jean plateau. This invincible phalanx was ready to brush everything before it. Nothing seemed to be able to stop it, not even the shot which was concentrated at it and cutting deep swathes among its ranks. But even this maddest of furies had to bow to the inevitable. Wellington faced them with everything he had left: the remnants from Ompteda's and Kielmansegge's brigades and especially those of Plat's and Maitland's, Adam's and Haskett's brigades which were still solid and determined, and the Chassé Brigade which arrived from Braine d'Alleud. The Guard could go no further. Suddenly the Red Coats thirty steps in front of them rose up and the bearskins were cut down by well-aimed salvoes from the Guards and the English Light Infantry. To the frightened cry of "the Guard is retreating!" the Imperial Army lost its hold. Wellington then ordered a general counter-attack as the Prussians swept through the last ranks of Lobau's Corps. Alone, the Old Guard, or what was left of it retreated in some form of order surrounded by its enemies which swarmed onto the battlefield. Infantrymen, cavalrymen and artillerymen tried to escape from the trap which was closing in on them, blocking the Charleroi road with indescribable chaos… Defeated, Napoleon forced his was through with great difficulty…

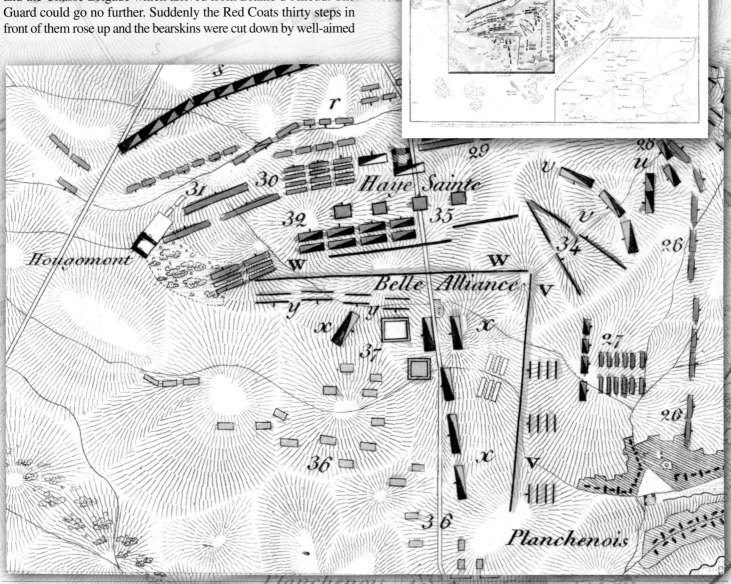

The last phalanx marches towards its destiny. A view of the battle by a modern artist: Giuseppe Rava. *Rights reserved*

VIVE L'EMPEREUR!

On the Pratzen Plateau on 2 December 1805, the warriors' acclaim had decided a brilliant victory. The Guard had entered history. Nine years later in the courtyard at the Chateau of Fontainbleau the same cry sadly saluted the Emperor's first departure towards exile. History could have stopped there. But the enthusiastic shouts from the Austerlitz "Grognards" were there again upon the return from exile at Elba. Finally it broke out amidst the English shot at Mont-Saint-Jean during the ultimate sacrifice. Did the Emperor realise that he would never hear it again?

Right.

A cartridge case belonging to a Grenadier of the Guard which came down to us only by complete luck. In Brabant, a local amateur had carefully collected its pieces. But the claws of the eagle clasping the thunder-flashes were missing. They reappeared rather a number of years later... The dedicated amateur was astonished to find them at the bottom of his cellar in a box he used to put his discoveries in many years earlier. It is sometimes in this manner that the vestiges from the past are patiently reconstructed.

Private Collection

From the spot where it fought its last battle, the Guard still occasionally delivers up a tiny vestige of its glorious death throes for us. The big buttons with a crowned eagle no doubt come from the Grenadiers' and the Chasseurs' blue greatcoat. The same eagle was also placed over the two crossed cannon of the artillery, as well as on this surprising button from the Ecole Spéciale Impériale Militaire which was used as a mere button in 1815.

Private Collection

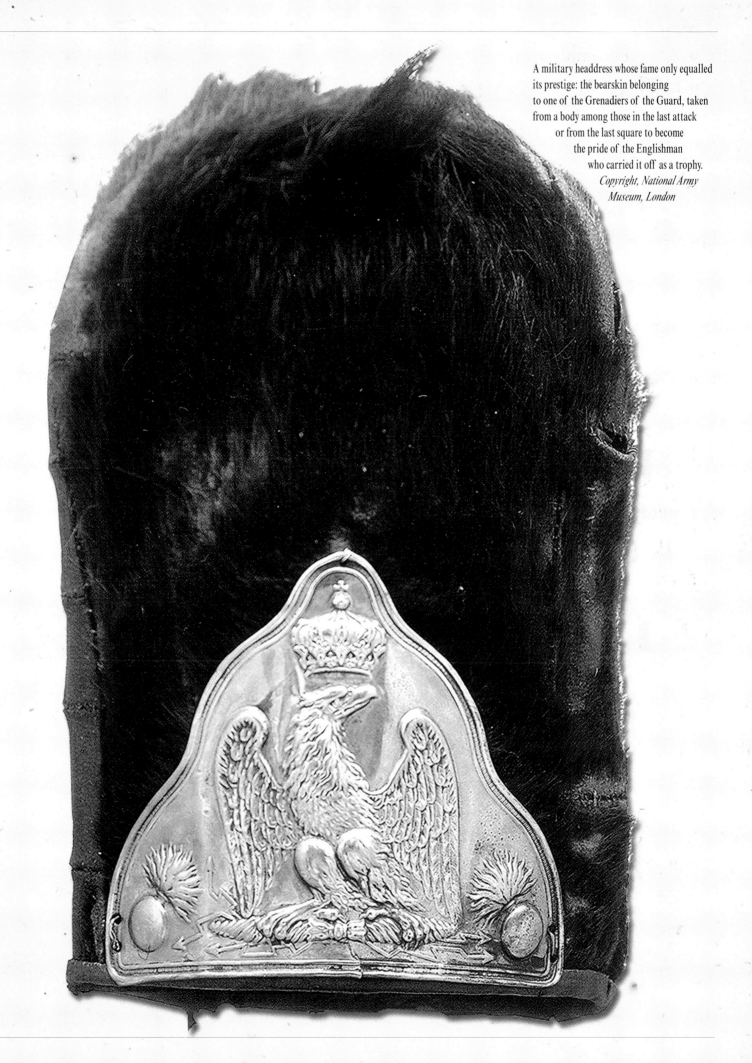

A military headdress whose fame only equalled
its prestige: the bearskin belonging
to one of the Grenadiers of the Guard, taken
from a body among those in the last attack
or from the last square to become
the pride of the Englishman
who carried it off as a trophy.
*Copyright, National Army
Museum, London*

The Guard starts to waver.
Composition by Eugène Leliêpvre. Private Collection

FRANCE
GRENADIERS A PIED.
GARDE IMPERIALE
WATERLOO – 18-6-1815

Badly oxidised and misshapen by their
long stay in the ground, these metal parts
of a sabre scabbard belonged
to an infantryman of the Guard.
Private Collection

HIS LORDSHIP RAISED HIS HAT

The Adam and Halkett Brigades had started the surge for-wards. Supported by Vandeleur's and Vivian's Cavalry, they tore down the slope between Hougoumont and la Haye-Sainte towards the last French squares. Wellington had understood that this was the moment when everything was about to sway. *"As matters stand, we may as well go right to the end; if the troops are advancing they may as well advance as far as they can"*, he said to Uxbridge. Putting his words into action, the Duke raised his hat on the point of his sword. Among the hurrahs of deliverance, all the valid men in the Low Countries Army started the victorious advance.

The Allies' counter-attack.
Painting by Knötel.
Rights Reserved

This aide de camp's uniform belonged to Captain Thomas Noel Harris who was wearing it when, in the ranks of the 18th Hussars in Vivian's Brigade, he charged the retreating Old Guard. Seriously wounded in the side by a bullet and by Biscayen shot in his right arm, he was only cared for on the following morning and had to be amputated on the spot at Hougoumont. He died... 45 years later full of honours. Ever since, his coat has been preserved by his descendants just as it was on the morrow of the battle with its sleeve open up to the collar, the bullet hole on the side and his blood stains mixed with those of glorious Waterloo mud.
Private Collection, Rights Reserved

Below.
A sabre belonging to Colonel Lane who fought in the ranks of the 15th Hussars in the 5th Brigade under Major-General Sir Colquhoun Grant. It was during the final attack by the Allied army that this brigade distinguished itself.
Copyright National Army Museum, London

The wounded Eagle.
Photo Gérard Lachaux, Rights Reserved

DERNIERS COMBATTANTS DE LA GRANDE ARMÉE

This sabretache belonging to a Chasseur à Cheval of the Guard is one of the most beautiful souvenirs from Waterloo, picked up as it was on the first day following the battle. The brightness of the colours has triumphed against time and enables us to catch a glimpse of the richness of the superb uniforms these Elite horsemen wore; one squadron protected the Emperor right up to the end.
Musée Royal de l'Armée Collection, Brussels

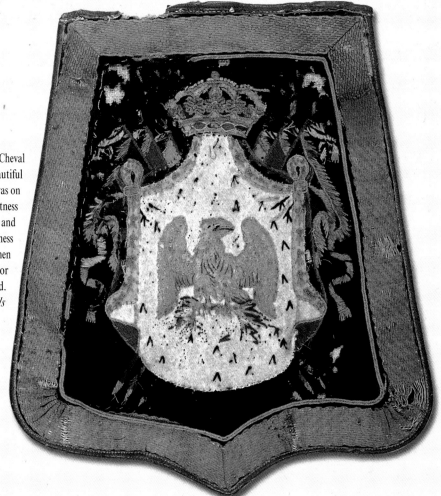

THE FLIGHT OF THE EAGLE

"Napoleon died at Waterloo. Having decided not to spare his army the massacre and to fall with it, he fell in among his Guard during its last moments of resistance. The silence of the grave fell upon men's fury. At the news of the unimaginable, the tides of the enemy could be seen to open up suddenly in front of the survivors of the last square. Taking their Emperor with them, the "Grognards" disappeared into the night in the face of their dazed enemy, disarmed by the magnitude of the event…"

All this is wrong, history just cannot be re-written like that! And yet… did the Emperor wish it so, in his heart of hearts? So many mistakes adding up all during that long fatal Sunday, were they worthy of such a great commander? Sensing that all was lost as soon as he realised that his most vehement enemy had outplayed him, did he not chose his own way out? What an end for a soldier like him, immolated by his own will in the middle of his destroyed army! With his own death, there would have been no winner on this field. Only Divine Will, beyond all understanding, would impose itself on men to perpetuate his memory. But his time had not yet come. With his flight, he was not going to sully his own legend, forged by his extraordinary spirit. In a few weeks' time, making up his mind all by himself as usual about the role he wanted to be his, he would know how to out-play the rest of Europe! By condemning him to quit the world, abandoned on his desolate island, the sovereigns did not understand that they were conferring immortality upon him.

Napoleon leaving the battlefield. At that very instant, he climbed onto Marengo, one of three horses used on 18 June. Abandoned to the English at le Caillou Farm, the horse died in London where one of his hooves was taken, just like Jock's from the 2nd Life Guards, and made into a tobacco box by Major Angerstein. Today it decorates the Officer's Mess of the Royal Guard at Saint-James' Palace.
Painting after Knötel

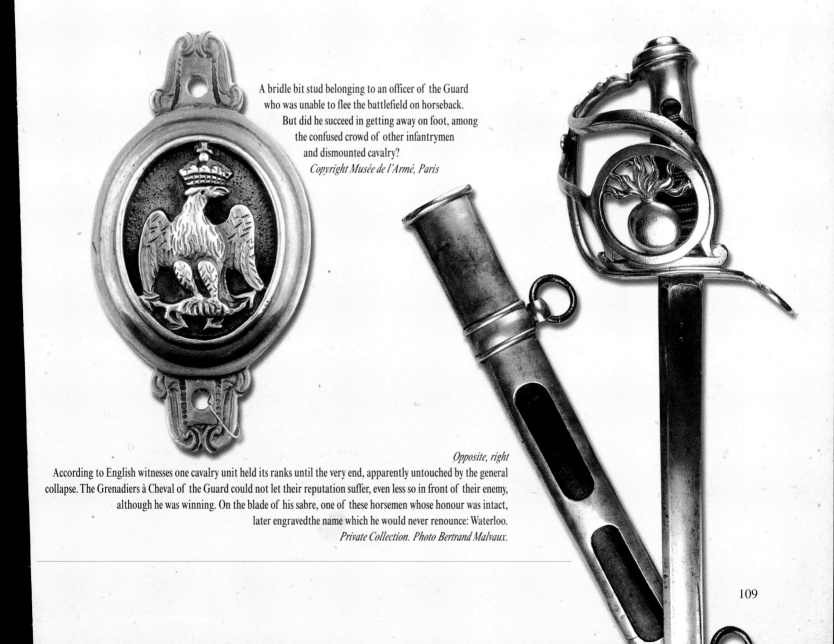

A bridle bit stud belonging to an officer of the Guard who was unable to flee the battlefield on horseback. But did he succeed in getting away on foot, among the confused crowd of other infantrymen and dismounted cavalry?
Copyright Musée de l'Armé, Paris

Opposite, right

According to English witnesses one cavalry unit held its ranks until the very end, apparently untouched by the general collapse. The Grenadiers à Cheval of the Guard could not let their reputation suffer, even less so in front of their enemy, although he was winning. On the blade of his sabre, one of these horsemen whose honour was intact, later engraved the name which he would never renounce: Waterloo.
Private Collection. Photo Bertrand Malvaux.

ON THE ROADS AFTER THE ROUT

It was all over, the Imperial Army had dissolved into chaos. Infantrymen, cavalry and artillerymen, all mixed up in incredible confusion tried to escape from their pursuers who were just as worn out as they were. Although fired by victory the victors barely had more energy than the crowd which was throwing down rifles and bags so as to be able to get away faster, abandoning the wounded and trampling under foot those who had the ill-luck to fall. Fear had taken hold of their minds, from the general to the last of the drummers; everybody was a law unto himself getting away, getting away as far as possible, getting away from the crushing tiredness which tore suffering from each step, getting away to save a life which it would be total madness to sacrifice now. What a horror they met at Quatre-Bras, coming across the sight of four thousand dead without a grave since 16 June met the flood of fleeing troops. Crushed by the dead men's silent reproach for such a senseless slaughter which quashed their fear, the deplorable herd left this place of terror. As distance and time brought the reassurance of safety, some got hold of themselves and regrouped around their Eagles. By some inexplicable mystery, not one was lost by that tattered army as it collapsed.

A Légion d'Honneur whose owner was on doubt worthy of wearing it; on the reverse of the Imperial Eagle there was the profile of good King Henri (IV) which reappeared under the First Restoration. To serve France no matter the regime, through all its glories and misfortunes, in victory as well as in defeat: this is what guided this officer's destiny right up to Waterloo, as it did for so many others.
Private Collection

This other Légion d'Honneur should have had pride of place in a frame in some brave soldier's house for his heirs. In 2000, the battlefield only handed back its twisted star, separated from its golden heart and the frail enamel. But is this not therefore more pathetic than the shiniest decoration in its velvet case?
Private Collection

More picturesque than moving, these two French stove escaped the darkness of time thanks to the Englishman's innate sense of preserving things. Curiosity or practical sense has this time guided the choice of some of Wellington's soldiers. The rustic ingeniousness of these copper utensils is still attractive today.
Copyright National Army Museum, London

Above.
Dead Cuirassier.
Detail from the Waterloo Panorama.

The cult of the Emperor affected most of his soldiers. Thus each of them carried some form of effigy representing the leader they adored. With his arms crossed in the well-known martial posture, this little bronze statuette or knife ornament had its place in a soldier's clobber. The Eagle's misfortune caused the loss of both man and effigy in the rout.
Musée "Dernier quartier général de Napoléon" collection.

From near le Caillou farm which was first the Emperor's Headquarters on the evening of 17 June, then the witness to his army's retreating survivors on the following day, this letter "N" from a fusilier's cartridge case has come to light 185 years later, by chance, when the earth was being ploughed for the last time in the 20th century.
Private Collection

French Prisoners
by Knötel.

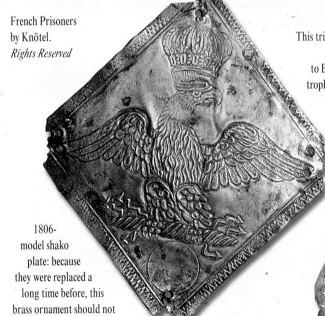

1806-
model shako
plate: because
they were replaced a
long time before, this
brass ornament should not
have been any of the
headdresses belonging to Waterloo combatants. For those
wanting to exploit them, the lessons learnt from studying a
battlefield are part of an exact science no matter what the rules
and their ardent supporters say.
Private Collection

Right.
This tricolour cockade which may have decorated
the bicorn hat of a French officer went
to England in a victor's luggage. A modest
trophy, but ever so symbolic - those colours
which the Allies had hoped to get rid
of once and for all!
*Copyright National Army Museum,
London*

The cartridge case has disappeared but the Eagle
What was this Hussar officer's fate?
Private Collection

For a long time now, "La Baleine", the French 6-pounder, has been in retirement in the hall of the Brussels museum, whereas its stable-mate, "La Suffisante", made in Douai in 1813, has been mounted on a new gun carriage in the Wellington Museum at Waterloo. These two pieces numbered among the 122 captured by the Army of the Low Countries.
Musée Royal de l'Armée, Brussels – Musée Wellington, Waterloo

After the horror of the battle there was the horror of the field hospital where, in very difficult conditions which one cannot imagine without a shudder, the Waterloo martyrs often underwent desperate operations. The saw and the trepan had pride of place in this casket belonging to a Belgian surgeon from Turnhout serving with the French. He was a Chevalier of the Légion d'Honneur and no doubt this health officer had been up to his superhuman task.
Private Collection

LORD UXBRIDGE'S LEG

Henry-William Paget, Lord Uxbridge, commanding the allied cavalry was wounded by one of the last cannonballs fired by the French artillery; it shattered his right knee. Carried to the Paris house, on the Brussels road at Waterloo where he had lodged the previous evening, he was amputated by the surgeon, John Powell. After bearing the operation with extraordinary courage, the phlegmatic aristocrat concluded the event with these words: *"I've had my time and I've been a beau for 47 years. It would not have been seemly to continue to compete with the young."* The illustrious invalid lived on until 1854.

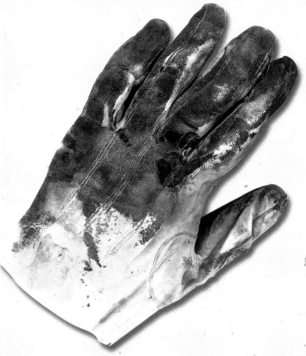

After being wounded, Lord Uxbridge was helped by his aide de camp Thomas Wildman of the 7th Hussars who saved his life by applying a tourniquet. As a souvenir of this dramatic moment, the officer kept his bloodied glove.
Copyright, National Army Museum, London

Left.
In the garden of the Wellington Museum at Waterloo one can now see hanging on a wall of the little building covered with tiles, the stele which once marked the grave of Uxbridge's leg which was at first buried behind the Paris house. These words can still be read: "This is the grave of Lord Uxbridge's leg, Pray for the rest of his body, I beg". Informed in 1878 that these bones which had been unearthed accidentally were the object of some macabre sightseeing, the Lord's descendants had them buried again in the Wellington cemetery. Perhaps to avoid a repetition of this improper curiosity, the burial took place with great discretion, so much so in fact that the bones were lost forever!
Photo Gérard Lachaux. Right reserved

Below.
The English habit of keeping everything is here again perfectly illustrated, since this saw is none other than the one used by John Powell to cut off the general's leg!
Copyright, National Army Museum, London

Below.
Even more prestigious is Lord Uxbridge's sabretache
which he was wearing on his left and which has come
down to us because as chance would have it,
the cannonball hit his right leg!
Copyright National Army Museum, London

Portrait of Lord Uxbridge

A PRÉDESTINÉD NAME

There is a modest tavern on the edge of the road in the direction of Charleroi, above the valley where the fate of the campaign was played out. With darkness falling hiding the terrible spectacle of the battlefield from the sight of the victors, the Duke of Wellington stopped his horse nearby. He was little inclined to show his feelings and listened imperturbably to the survivors of the regimental bands playing "*God save the King*" to celebrate the victory which had been won so dearly. From the depths towards Plancenoit, the Prussians emerged like a huge church procession chanting the old Lutheran hymn "*Herr Gott Dich loben wir! Herr Gott wir danken Dir!*" A group of horsemen approached in the night. The Commander in Chief of the Army of the Low Countries recognised Marshal Blücher among them. The two Commanding Officers congratulated each other and exchanged a few words… in French! In the great confusion of the moment, their meeting was almost miraculous. The name of the place ought to be known. Somebody mentioned "La Belle-Alliance". Moved by the symbolism, the Prussian suggested to his alter ego that they should name their victory after it. But in the end the other imposed the name of the village where his headquarters were situated and which sounded more English to him, and this was more pleasing to the ear.

Left.
Near Rossomme, one of the victors lost this button from a shoulder flap. The Roman figure indicates that it belonged to a Grenadier from the 1st Battalion of a Prussian regiment.
Private Collection

Left.
The Prussian monument built in 1818 bears this inscription in German: "*To the fallen heroes, the King and the grateful country. Belle-Alliance, 18 June 1815.*"
As the first country to commemorate its victory on the spot, Prussia confirmed its preference for the name chosen by Marshal Blücher to celebrate the Allies' victory.
Photo Gérard Lachaux, Rights Reserved

Above and right
From Saint-Cloud to Waterloo, the story of a Sabre of Honour. Where was it put on show, together with its label written by the buyer who paid his twelve napoleons? From seller to buyer, everybody must have got something out of it.
Musée Royal de l'Armée, Brussels

116

This sabre-knot found on the battlefield once belonged to a Prussian officer from the 2nd Regiment of the Queen's Dragoons. Belonging to the Cavalry reserves of the 1st Corps under von Ziethen, he came into contact with the French after 7 p.m. and thus hardly fought at Waterloo. A very old repair gives us the solution to the enigma: its ribbon was torn and the owner did not even realise that he had lost it in the growing dusk.
Musée Napoléon de Ligny Collection

Right.
A French tourist sent this post card to Paris on 25 May 1906. Inside the farm one can see that the memory of the Emperor is carefully preserved with a full-size statue. But legend reminds us that the spot was also where Blücher and Wellington came across each other.
Private Collection

Waterloo. — Intérieur de la Belle Alliance où se rencontraient Blücher et Wellington.

IN WATERLOO'S EARTH

Soon two centuries will have gone by since that terrible day in June 1815 and yet the battlefield still reveals some of its relics. Far from the madding crowd of auction rooms and antique exhibitions, some amateurs still search untiringly all over the fields, where there are now no longer any traces of the slaughter... If one is really determined and patient enough, a miracle can still happen: in the recently ploughed earth, the round grey shape of a bullet comes to light, a green trace of oxide can announce an interesting discovery. Is it a button? And the searcher's feverish thumb tries to get the regimental number to appear. He is often disappointed... But each fragment brought into the light of day is an infinitesimal part of the battle. A bit of shako plate and the amateur historian can reconstruct the soldier's hat, can imagine the soldier himself and make him advance once more to meet his fate. Finding relics at Waterloo, is like delving into the heart of memory...

Present day view of part of the battlefield, of la Haie-Sainte at Frichemont, taken from near la Belle-Alliance where Napoleon once stood.
Photo Gérard Lachaux – Rights Reserved

IN THE SHADOW
OF THE BUTTE DU LION

It can be seen miles away, no matter where one is coming from. Never had such an impressive landmark been erected on a battlefield. Today the Butte du Lion is the tourists' assembly point. Latter-day Cotton counterparts propose an abundance of souvenirs, brochures and figurines made some distance from the historic site. What is it possible to find which could be more authentic? When they climb this great earthen cone, these passers-by cannot even imagine that they are treading on a whole mystery of bronze, of bones and iron - Waterloo's real memory at half an elbow's length from their shoes.

Right.
Bullets and shell bursts
"… The surrounding
ground was so sodden by
the rain that in certain
cases the shells dug
themselves into the
ground, under the surface and
when they exploded they threw up
mud and sand all over the place and
were comparatively harmless.
However, the older soldiers had never witnessed such
a furious artillery barrage."
Major Edward Cotton, "A voice from Waterloo",
Private Collection

Above and left.
One can reasonably assume
that most of the
breastplates littering
the 18 June battlefield
were picked up quickly
in the following days.
This exception is oxidised,
showing how long a time it spent
in the ground. The two shoulder scales accompanying it might even
have belonged to it. They were found by a lucky walker in 1965 whose
eye was attracted to a small stain of verdigris right at the foot
of the Butte du Lion…
Musée Royal de l'Armée, Brussels and Private Collection

Right.
Firecaps and lead vice-blocks. One of these appeared on
top of a lump of earth, clearly visible just after a
storm; it was if it was proffered just to the person who
would know how to discover it.
Private Collection

Below.
Detail from the Waterloo Panorama.
Photo Gérard Lachaux, Rights Reserved

THE WATERLOO BUTTONS:
THE IMPERIAL ARMY LAST PARADE

Waterloo was not a war game… Today, the complex organisation of the regiments, the squadrons and the batteries is unendingly reconstituted by the specialists with life's colours but in truth, the now legendary real uniforms had a very undignified end on the day after the battle. The dead were frantically stripped of their uniforms because cloth was such a rare commodity. All that was not usable – which was not very much after all – was burnt on the pyre or left to rot in the ground. The jacket-coats, the dolmans, the overcoats from Waterloo only left their buttons behind, cut off in the height of the battle. The curious amateur can make something of these buttons because often their numbers or symbols revealed their origin. Recognised by his unit, the infantrymen, the troopers or the gunners recover their places in the unchanging battle order of 18 June. But all rules have their exceptions and these often perturb budding wargame Napoleons who, ensconced within their totally military logic, have not yet learnt that the tortuous realities of all the little details of history can contradict the rules they have learnt.

Above.
Nine French buttons carefully and secretly preserved in a collector's drawer. Those with an Eagle are from the Artillery or Infantry of the Guard, and those with a number of a Line regiment pose no problem. On the other hand, that of the 7th Artillery does, as it was theoretically not there at Waterloo but the button was nevertheless found there, as was its neighbour with the fleur-de-lys. The latter being present is not particularly surprising as a good number of the combatants must have kept this type of button because they had to or because they had no particular desire to change them.
Private Collection

Below.
Although seemingly incongruous, the presence of Navy Artillery buttons can be more easily explained. Some of these men had the redoubtable privilege of being used as reinforcements for the batteries of the Guard, before the Army of the North started its campaign. *Private Collection*

Above.
At Waterloo, one cannot always believe what these buttons seem to reveal. None of these regiments set foot anywhere near Waterloo. The 112th, 117th, 142nd, 151st and 153rd were disbanded during the First Restoration. The Colonial Battalions distinguished themselves in other places. Who was responsible for these incongruous buttons being there? And the uniforms, reassigned soldiers?
Private Collection

Left.
The French troops seen from the Allied lines. Detail from the Waterloo Panorama.
Photo Gérard Lachaux, Rights Reserved

HISTORY'S HARVEST

The first days of the third millennium… The immense fields with lazy folds have forgotten the distant and fleeting 18 June. For as far as one can see, there is nothing. However, over in the distance a little black silhouette is moving along the invisible furrows. It stops, bends over then starts off again on its mysterious quest. This solitary walker is slowly crossing the tragic spot where the 1st Corps under the Comte d'Erlon was broken up by the enemy cavalry. For years, this man has made it his duty to pick up the slightest clues to the few hours of a drama which is now eternal. A lifetime's patience has borne its fruits…

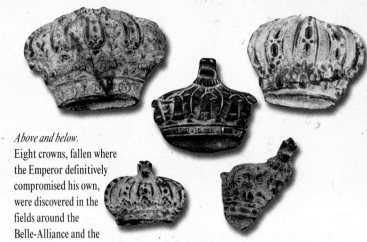

Above and below.
Eight crowns, fallen where the Emperor definitively compromised his own, were discovered in the fields around the Belle-Alliance and the Mont-Saint-Jean crossroads. It is difficult to say what they were for: ornaments for headdress, cartridge cases, sabretaches or baldrics…
Private Collection

Patiently sifted out throughout the seasons, countless little copper or bronze objects have accumulated in the collections of individuals who constantly roam the battlefield. It is sometimes almost impossible to identify each discovery with accuracy. In the middle of the various carriers, buckles and ornaments, at the top, on the right there is a watch winder, decorated with a Masonic insignia; and beside it an officer's tie pin. The smaller of the two grenades shown here was with three other similar ones surrounding an Eagle, on the flap of a cartridge case belonging to a Grenadier of the Guard.
Private Collections

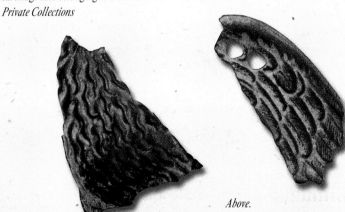

Above.
Two fragments of feather, almost nothing…
This was the shako eagle of a French officer.
The historian reconstitutes it in his thoughts…
Private Collection

THE HUMBLE TREASURES BELONGING TO THE FALLEN

The man walked up to us with an assured step, along the furrows of plough - his universe. He opened his calloused hand: there appeared two little verdigris disks and four lead balls covered with clay. Nothing more trivial for this Brabant man. What is more, in his home, he has piously preserved a moving collection of relics patiently obtained from the soil, broken up a hundred-fold by the share. Luckily for us, he opened the gate to this secret garden of his…

History in the hollow of the hand.

Above.
Two tap spindles from a tun: one is British, shaped like a dolphin; the other is French, shaped like a cock. They evoke the mess wagons which followed the campaigning armies.
Private Collection

Knucklebones and dice were the most popular games for soldiers when billeted or camping. The dreadful apprehension while they waited between 17 and 18 June, in Belle-Alliance's sodden fields, did not exactly encourage absorbing rounds of dice and knucklebones!
Private Collection

Detail from the Waterloo Panorama.
Photo Gérard Lachaux. Rights Reserved

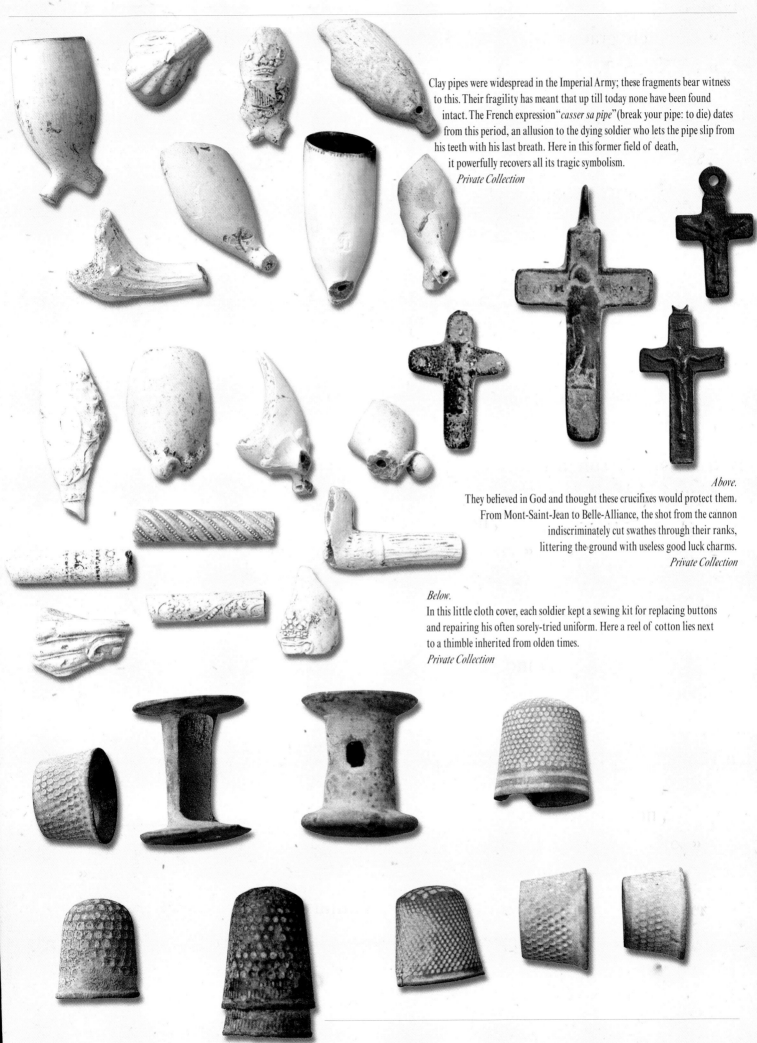

Clay pipes were widespread in the Imperial Army; these fragments bear witness to this. Their fragility has meant that up till today none have been found intact. The French expression "*casser sa pipe*" (break your pipe: to die) dates from this period, an allusion to the dying soldier who lets the pipe slip from his teeth with his last breath. Here in this former field of death, it powerfully recovers all its tragic symbolism.
Private Collection

Above.
They believed in God and thought these crucifixes would protect them. From Mont-Saint-Jean to Belle-Alliance, the shot from the cannon indiscriminately cut swathes through their ranks, littering the ground with useless good luck charms.
Private Collection

Below.
In this little cloth cover, each soldier kept a sewing kit for replacing buttons and repairing his often sorely-tried uniform. Here a reel of cotton lies next to a thimble inherited from olden times.
Private Collection

Below.
The only shine which time has not dimmed: gold. Very occasionally, offering itself to sight and greed, it glitters occasionally in the mud which here revealed these two coins.
Private Collection

Right.
Silver coins, bronze coins: those who were unable to spend them paid for their unattainable victory with their lives.
Private Collection

Inaugurated in 1913, this modest ossuary holds the remains of the combatants found almost a century later. "*Pro Imperator saepe, pro patria sempre.*" - Often for the Emperor, always for the Motherland. Such is the motto inscribed on its pediment. With these few words, Hector Fleichmann and Lucien Landy, the designers of the monument wanted to pay tribute to those who according to the initial sense of the expression, gave up their lives and lie in these massed graves. But the Latin's ambiguity suggests that perhaps former enemies now lie at rest with each other.
Photo Gérard Lachaux, Rights Reserved

Last view of the Eagle…
Private Collection

Opposite page.
"The Guard dies…" Drawing by Job.
Private Collection

The authors would express their thanks to the following for their help in preparing this work:

Alain Arq, Catherine Baranger, Léon Bernard, Hervé Bernard, François Binétruy, Marc Bouxin, Philippe de Calataÿ, Béatrice de Chancel-Bardelot, Piet de Gryse, Jacques Declercq, Roger Delpierre, Charly Delroisse, Jean-Claude Dey, Pierre D'Harville, Luc Frère, K. C. Hughes, Pierre Juhel, Christina La Torre, Michel Lefèbvre, Eugène Lelièpvre, Jacques Logie, Bertrand Malvaux, Gilbert Menne, André Moriau, Hermann Plote, Giuseppe Rava, André-Charles Sonmereyn, Pierre Verly, Ernst Ludwig Wagner.

May they receive here the thanks they deserve.

Giuseppe Rava
www.militaryart.it

Editing by Denis Gandilhon
Design and lay-out by Antoine Poggioli.
© Histoire & Collections 2005

ISBN: 2-915239-69-X

Publisher's number: 2-915239

© Histoire & Collections 2005

A book from
Histoire & Collections
SA au capital de 182 938, 82 €
5, avenue de la République
F-75541 Paris Cedex 11
Téléphone 01 40 21 18 20
Fax   01 47 00 51 11
www.histoireetcollections.fr

This book has been designed, typed, laid-out and processed by *Histoire & Collections* and *le Studio Graphique A & C* on fully integrated computer equipment. Color separation by the Studio A&C Printed by ZURE, Spain, European Union December 2005.